DEATH OF A LEGEND

DEATH OF A LEGEND

Summer of '72

Team Canada
vs. USSR Nationals

Edited
and written
by Henk W. Hoppener

The Copp Clark Publishing Company
Montreal   Toronto   Winnipeg   Vancouver

Foreword

Each of us has her or his own memories of the *Team Canada v. USSR Nationals* series. It has been called "the hockey series of the century." Ardent Canadian fans agree that it was, and objective spectators will admit that the claim is one of the less exaggerated aspects of the event. The series permitted us to see hockey as most of us had never seen it before. But the games demonstrated more than excellent hockey; they were much more than a thrilling sport's contest. Conflicting systems, cultures and values were as much a part of the series as were the games themselves.

This book presents a selection of images and impressions recorded during the series by some of Canada's best photographers and writers. It represents one man's choice of words and pictures which best illustrate the things he would like to remember. It also reflects how Canadians displayed and observed symbols of their nationhood, unique features of Canadian nationalism.

Several comments, including those written by the editor, have more to do with Canadian identity and purpose than with hockey. Yet, without the memorable series, these comments would not have been made and without the events which provoked the comments, the series would not have been memorable.

Death of a Legend is a scrapbook of memories as well as a record of some of the things Canadians seemed to be thinking and saying about themselves in the late summer of '72.
H.W.H.

Whatever Happened to Hockey?

The summer of '72. A Russian summer it was. In Canada the harvest looked poor, unemployment high, inflation progressive. A general election was called. There was murder in Munich, mayhem in the Middle East, and mass-defection from McGovern. Whatever else happened in Canada, or in the world, seemed to mean little in comparison with the *Team Canada — USSR Nationals* hockey series.

It seems fair to say that nothing excited so many Canadians as deeply as the hockey series; nothing drew as much interest or aroused as much emotion in the country and its institutions. On the surface it seemed no more than a sports contest between a team of Canadians and a team of Russians; but surface appearances were deceptive — as deceptive as ice.

In the scheme of things, international sports encounters occur frequently enough to become commonplace; incidents of passing interest. They are, at most, multiple versions of the ancient Roman circus. Not so with hockey — not in Canada. The series was not to be seen as a matter of passing interest, on the surface or off it. Nothing less than nationhood was being put to the test on several important counts.

By universal definition, a nation is a group of people linked by common experience, sharing common goals, identifying with common values. As a nation so defined, Canada has been having a hard time lately sensing and demonstrating its nationhood. Canadians have had few assists to nationhood through history. Canada's geography, once a challenge to settlers and railroad builders, is little more today than a barrier compounded by distance. Nature itself conspires by driving most Canadians to ground for long seasons of cold discontent and dispersing them to escape the short, fierce blasts of summer.

National unity, integrity and purpose are abstract political propositions that lose out to bread and butter. They are not causes that give Canadians living heroes.

But, for years, the majority of Canadians have been united at least in their irrepressible belief that hockey was their cause, their common fascinating attraction, their visible symbol of pre-eminence in the world. While their counterparts in the U.S. may aspire to stardom in baseball, business, or politics, countless youngsters in Canada clothe their vision of greatness in a hockey uniform and crown their ambitions with a helmet. There probably is not a Canadian male alive who has not at some time put on a pair of skates and held a hockey stick in the midst of a

dreary winter . . . and dreamed of greatness. There probably is not a television program in the world which has as high and as loyal a per-capita rating of viewers as *Hockey Night in Canada*. There is no subject in Canadian public life which so many people can discuss knowledgeably and intensively as "last night's game." Hockey fans are Canada's greatest classless mass. Hockey's folklore, myths and mystique make up the main body of all-Canadian culture. Hockey has become an affair of state, a prop of nationhood. It may have taken some time, but even the Canadian government has begun in recent years to understand the phenomenon and to make it an instrument of policy.

And so, when on the second day of September 1972, more than 12 million people in Canada gathered in front of their television sets to watch Game One of the *Team Canada — USSR Nationals* series, something vital to the nation was happening. This was far more than a new hockey season which had arrived early; far more than the unfolding of a new episode in the national weekly hockey drama. It was the culmination of two years of planning and preparation for a confrontation and a confirmation; the moment of truth; the culmination of a galling and frustrating debate which had begun years earlier, when a Canadian national team for the first time lost an international hockey championship and caused Canadians and the world to doubt our most visible claim to superiority. The initial doubt grew stronger. After the first loss, we found, as year succeeded year, that good, strong, winning hockey was being played by the Soviets, the Czechs, the Swedes, the East Germans, and so on. We tried comeback after comeback with every means at our command. We hoped, prayed, fumed and fussed. But our losing streak continued and our anxiety grew. We began by objecting that the foreigners were not amateurs, and by ignoring our own doubtful claim to amateur status in the accepted meaning of the word. Then, at last, we withdrew from international competition, and in doing so disturbed ourselves more than we disturbed the world. In our ultimate frustration, we challenged any foreign team, but especially the Russian champions, to meet and beat a team of Canada's best — a team we had not been able to field under international rules.

The Soviets finally accepted our challenge; ironically, after they had lost the world championship to the Czechs.

Earlier, the Canadian government had set up a task force, a supreme investigating body, to report on the state of sports in Canada. The emphasis in the report was on hockey, and the thrust of its recommendations was aimed at no less than a major government effort to "save" hockey, the national game . . .

The Canadian government created and financed Hockey Canada and assigned to this institution the responsibility of promoting and improving hockey by and for Canadians. Hockey Canada in turn created *Team Canada*. It did so with the cooperation of the Canadian Amateur Hockey Association which is the official, national governing body of amateur hockey in Canada. The role of the CAHA in this instance was limited primarily to obtaining agreement from its Soviet counterpart and from the International Ice Hockey Federation to the staging of the Canada — USSR series. The International Federation is accredited by the International Olympic Committee as the world governing body of amateur hockey.

The CAHA had little or nothing to do with organizing the series or selecting *Team Canada*. It benefits financially, as does the International Federation at least to the extent of collecting a heavy sanctioning fee. The CAHA has financial and legal ties with the NHL whose governors are predominantly foreign. In legal parlance it can be said that there have been and remain many parties to every part of the series, though none that does only Canada's bidding.

In July 1972, the coach, assistant coach and the thirty-five NHL players selected for *Team Canada* were announced by the chairman of Hockey Canada Douglas Fisher. Present at the ceremony were also government representatives, CAHA representatives, and Mr. Alan Eagleson, executive director of the NHL Players' Association, and agent for a number of individual hockey players. Mr. Eagleson appeared capable of representing more interests than a chameleon is capable of changing colours. As it turned out, Mr. Eagleson was the kingpin and power broker in the affair.

The announcement of the *Team Canada* selection rocked the peaceable dominion and threw the usually tranquil administration of hockey into an uproar the likes of which few Canadians had ever before seen or taken part in. The uproar was caused by the revelation that only players with NHL club contracts could be members of *Team Canada*. This condition, stipulated in an agreement made many months earlier by the NHL and Hockey Canada, prevented one of the most popular and one of the greatest players of all time, Bobby Hull, from joining the selects. (The public has not seen evidence of the agreement; Mr. Eagleson's word must be taken that it was made.)

It seems strange that the Hull controversy stopped as suddenly as it had started especially on considering that no other incident, no act or fact, no statement associated with the two-year period in which the Canada — USSR hockey series was being prepared or with the decades in which Canada's hockey history was plagued with misfortune — nothing had provoked the kind of attention raised by the Hull affair. Comment from both officials and the news media was confined almost exclusively to the control exerted by the NHL and Mr. Eagleson to prevent Bobby Hull from playing — there was no demand for

reasons which might be acceptable to Canadians; for justifications based on Canadian law; for an enquiry into the effects on Canadian sovereignty.

There was comment, in the news media, at least, that the agreement with the NHL had been a mistake, a necessity to obtain the League's cooperation, an innocent clause which had been stipulated long before anyone could anticipate that the World Hockey Association might be a source of competition. The agreement, it was argued, was a means of obtaining the best players while fully protecting them and their interests. There are few cases in Canadian public life which are clearer illustrations of the ends justifying the means.

Whatever happened to hockey? Whatever possessed Canadians in the summer of 72?

The game of hockey though it did not originate in Canada, was once played by hundreds of thousands of Canadians for its own sake — as a competitive sport — nothing more nor less. That game over the years has become the property of big foreign business for the sole purpose of making a profit. That fact and its implications are being ignored by Canadians in their preoccupation with the hockey spectacle.

There is ample evidence that Canadian youngsters who show talent as hockey players are unable to play their sport after reaching high school age unless they join the professional system or are willing to suffer the frustration of muddled, disorganized mediocrity. Only local initiative in some parts of Canada and some school and college hockey offer competitive sport for the sake of sport. The rest of the hockey scene is dominated by business interests that reserve their backing to buy the allegiance of the CAHA and of young Canadians who dream and strive for NHL stardom.

The Canadian government has been aware of the situation for some time. It has been informed by a recent task force and before that by the National Advisory Committee on Fitness and Amateur Sport — to name only two major sources — that hockey the sport and hockey the business do not mix; that the sport of hockey should be governed by Canadians for the sole benefit of Canadian youngsters.

The advisory committee, having been asked by the federal government in 1966 to examine amateur hockey in Canada, made the following among many other recommendations:

We strongly recommend that the federal government of Canada initiate legislation in whatever form it deems most suitable which will achieve the purpose of guaranteeing to amateur hockey freedom from any kind of interference from the National Hockey League or its agents.

We recommend that provincial governments consider the enactment of legislation for the protection of young athletes of 18

By Our Hockey the World Shall Know Us

Uluschak — The Edmonton Journal

years and under from contracts with professional hockey which will in any way interfere with their pursuit of amateur hockey interests, their education, or their moral and physical well-being.

We recommend that in order to build a competent national team all amateur players in Canada, either drafted or not drafted by professional teams, must be given the right to play for the national team if they so desire.

Six years ago, one could still speak of hockey as a sport and respect the ambition of amateurs to play excellent hockey. It then seemed possible to hold the NHL at bay and to keep a sense of proportion. In the intervening years professional hockey has become synonymous with excellence in absolute terms; it has also become the only avenue for regaining world superiority.

Hockey superiority has become a Canadian obsession. It has blurred Canadian values and our sense of proportion to such an extent that the moguls of the NHL have been allowed to become the impressarios of what we consider our birthright and symbol of nationhood.

Is this the way to conduct the nation's business? Never have Canadians asked this question as often as in recent years, when pride in independence and the rejection of foreign ownership, controls and influence have become serious, growing public concerns. The content of textbooks and television programs keep intelligent people busy mounting repatriation campaigns. Yet, clearly no cause or property considered Canadian, rightly or wrongly, has as large and evident a vested Canadian interest as hockey. And for this cause we beg and borrow authority which we do not control; we accept conditions which compromise

Canadian laws, statutes, sportsmanship, self-respect, our sense of humor and just about everything else that is right and good.

It isn't as if hockey has elevated us from obscurity to the status of a world power. It isn't as if the universe has come to a halt to watch us show our stuff on a few square yards of ice. Our status as a nation does not hang on the outcome of a hockey game. What is it that makes us so unreasonable when it comes to hockey?

We win or lose hockey by winning or losing games. Whatever happened to hockey in any other context and for any other reason should not lead us into national madness and collective self-delusion. Or should it? Have we found in our hockey shock some hallucinogenic substitute for a game, admittedly of great appeal to Canadians and very much a part of our culture, but a game all the same . . . just a game?

We insist that by our hockey the world shall know us. Pity the world if it cared a damn, and damn the world if it were to care. Pity ourselves if whatever happened to hockey has happened to us.

Let's hope that it only looked that way in the summer of '72.

H.W.H.

The Hull-abaloo

Bobby Hull is human. Hit him and he hurts. Bash him and he bleeds. Ban him and he burns with frustration.

He has two arms, two legs, and two of everything else characteristic of most human males. He is so human that he has lost a few teeth in violent encounters with the tools of his trade. If you believe everything you read, some prematurely bald worry-spots in his fair curls have been repaired with a hair transplant.

A hero to millions, Bobby Hull is also a pied piper, a turn-coat and a wrong-faith evangelist to some. After 15 years in the National Hockey League, he is one of its all-time greats: fast, strong, skilful. Graceful and charming, he is a winner on and off the ice.

The trouble with Bobby was that early in July two employers claimed him as their very own. The Chicago Black Hawks claimed that Hull's contract with them ran until the end of September. They also argued that by prior agreement only players with NHL contracts for the current season were eligible for *Team Canada* duties. The second employer, the Winnipeg Jets and the new World Hockey Association, signed Hull and gave him one million dollars as a down-payment for his services as player-coach and public-relations agent. Because of this conflict, a third employer, the Canadian tax payers' *Team Canada*, had to deny Bobby the opportunity to moonlight among the stars against the national team of the Soviet Union.

The star of shooting stars was kept out of orbit on the orders of a Chicago judge, and when it became known that Bobby Hull would not be on *Team Canada*, public and official furor erupted across the nation as it had seldom erupted before. Much was said and written in anger more than in sorrow. The Prime Minister cabled Clarence Campbell. The minister of National Health and Welfare, sponsor of *Team Canada*, first spoke hopeful, then bitter words. Letters to the editor that got into print were furious; one shudders to think what the contents were of those that didn't.

Douglas Fisher, one-time politician, journalist and boss of *Hockey Canada*, was unusually diplomatic and tended to waffle. Mr. Alan Eagleson, lawyer, backroom politician, and boss of the NHL Players' Association, sounded unusually disturbed. He accused the Prime Minister of playing politics with the Hull affair. The United Church, meeting in annual conference, was unusually critical and made statements about Mammon, obscene greed, and patriotism. The Royal Canadian Legion remained silent. Pierre Berton spoke. Mr. Clarence Campbell, president of

the NHL, did not lose his cool in public, but he was heard to mutter uncustomary language after a commercial break in a television show on which he appeared. He also said that he would meet the Prime Minister "as a minimum courtesy." Evidently, the P.M. knew that he was licked; the courtesy no matter how minimal was not invited.

Team Canada selects were to be the best, the very best, players. They were to be Canadians all. By agreement, hammered out many months earlier, all players were to hold signed contracts with an NHL club. Bobby Hull was missing when training camp opened in Toronto in "the house of Harold Ballard," otherwise known as Maple Leaf Gardens. Mr. Ballard, involved as he was in some personal trouble with the law, spoke up for Bobby's participation. It was a courageous stand, especially courageous in that Mr. Ballard is one of only two Canadian NHL owners. When Clarence Campbell, strictly speaking Mr. Ballard's hireling, reportedly suggested that the Maple Leaf owner's court conviction nullified his role as a governor of the NHL, it took some clear thinking to determine from Toronto reports whether or not Ballard was perhaps a greater victim than Bobby Hull. Bobby came off a winner in the money department at least. Ballard, finding no favour with his NHL colleagues, was forced to give ground but remained, nevertheless, a jovial and generous host to the training camp held in his stadium.

If for Ballard, money had acquired a sudden tendency to turn to ashes, for Bobby Hull, anything he seemed to touch was coming up roses. Millionnaire Hull, by the fiscal yardstick, carried the highest price tag of any absentee from *Team Canada*. There were other absentees. Bobby Orr, darling of Boston groupies, could not make it because of a knee operation. He brought cheer and moral support to training camp on a near-corpulent 210-pound frame. Others had failed to sign their contracts with the NHL, or had defected to the WHA.

The Hull-abaloo owed more to expressions of national insecurity, anxiety, and emotion than to logic or objective analysis. A case in point is a column by Jim Vipond, usually a wise and eloquent commentator, who is sports editor of the Toronto *Globe and Mail*.

"If *Team Canada* is to have any meaning at all and this country is to be represented by the best hockey players we have, Bobby Hull must play. There can be no logical argument against his selection to the team to play Russia.

"Granted the National Hockey League has been most co-operative in making players available. Granted also that league president Clarence Campbell did a major job in persuading dissident governors of the predominantly U.S. controlled organization that all Canadian-born players, regardless of team affiliation should be made available.

"But *Team Canada* is not a commercial venture. It is a

national team organized to play a series of matches against the best side Russia can present. The series of eight matches will be exhibition in name only. Russia has prepared long and well for this challenge. Canada should not take it lightly.

"Competition between the NHL and the World Hockey Association, a new group which until quite recently the NHL has refused to recognize should have no bearing on selection of players.

"Professional hockey is big financial business. Club owners invest millions to make a profit. The players in the NHL bargain as best they can, restricted as they are by the legal weapon known as the reserve clause.

"Now a new league comes along with sacks full of money and the players are termed traiters because they prefer $250,000 to $50,000. That's the name of the game that the money-conscious NHL governors get fat on. Why shouldn't their serfs do the same?

"They don't want Bobby Hull to play for *Team Canada* because he was an astute enough businessman to realize that his playing days are limited and he has an opportunity to make some big money.

"He'll probably be joined any day now by New York's Brad Park and Boston's Gerry Cheevers, both considering offers beyond their wildest imaginations. Will they be banned too if they sign WHA contracts. According to Mr. Campbell's interpretation of the rules they'll not see Moscow in the fall.

"Once again Canada will not be sending its best team against the Russians, despite *Team Canada* coach Harry Sinden's reasonable suggestion he could have selected another 35 players just about as good as his first squad. But not quite, Harry. You know second best is not good enough.

"This is not the time for bickering. If the NHL is the big-league organization it claims to be, it should not hesitate to inform Hockey Canada that it will agree to amend the terms of reference to include the best players regardless of affiliation. It should be a matter of pride.

"Gentlemen of the National Hockey League, save the infighting for later. Don't ruin a good thing. Act today. Let everyone know that Bobby Hull is more than welcome. You'll have all year to fight with the WHA. The Russian challenge may not come again for a long time."

Given the tone of the discussion (which was pretty rough by any Canadian newspaper standards) Mr. Vipond's lines were measured. But logical and consistent? What possible reason could twelve U.S. NHL owners have to commiserate with us on the decline of Canadian hockey in the international arena? What evidence was there to suggest that the *Team Canada* operation was not a commercial venture? A fat lot of money was involved and a victorious performance by *Team Canada* was bound to benefit not only NHL teams but also the WHA teams, most

of which are based on Canadian territory. As for matters of pride and national self-esteem, these surely could only concern Canadians, and could hardly appeal to U.S. club owners who, as Mr. Vipond correctly stated, view hockey in terms of a business in which they invest millions to make a profit. Next to hockey, our greatest national sport has become raising hell about U.S. ownership of Canada. Can we ignore the rules of that particular sport and appeal to our opponents for access to "property" that they legitimately own, control and operate within their own borders? Possessed as he was by his concern to preserve our national pride, Mr. Vipond lost touch for a moment with a sense of reality and proportion.

More realistically, the *Ottawa Citizen* joined the Hull-abaloo with a lead editorial which said in part:

"Hockey Canada, which entered into that despicable agreement which will keep Bobby Hull from playing for his country against the Russian national team this fall, is a creation of the federal government. In fact specifically Health Minister Munro. The most unconscionable part of the agreement is not that Bobby Hull will be unable to play for Canada, as bad as that may be.

"What is more deplorable is that the weight of the nation's prestige, and the sports fans' fervor are being used to beat a player into signing a contract with his NHL employer. Nobody seriously expects Bobby Hull to give up $2 million. What of the player who may be coerced into accepting a bad contract just so he can clear himself to play for his country? The principle is the same — and should never have been agreed to, particularly by an agency of the federal government.

"Could we not at least eliminate the hypocrisy by renaming it Team NHL, instead of *Team Canada?*"

In the *Toronto Star*, Milt Dunnell found the NHL Players' Association, of which Bobby Hull was not a member, more to blame than the NHL owners. He suggested that the players collectively could have put sufficient pressure on the owners to make them relent. "But it left Hull at the bank, counting his money . . ." Dunnell believes he knows the reasons. Hull apparently was not on the friendliest of terms with the players and their benefactor, Alan Eagleson. Hull had frequently criticized the Players' Association, and according to Milt Dunnell, Hull had wanted one thirty-fifth of the income from the hockey series against the Soviets to be paid into the WHA players' pension fund.

Another writer, Vic Grant of the *Winnipeg Tribune*, evidently in disagreement with Mr. Vipond in Toronto, wrote: "Somebody should take the initiative and tell Hockey Canada that it is not to Bobby Hull's benefit that he plays, but to *Team Canada's* benefit . . . Hockey Canada's original concept has long been forgotten and this international show is strictly a money-making proposition

now . . ." This bit of rhetorical redundancy may have raised some eyebrows. After all, just about everybody had taken some initiative to tell Hockey Canada all kinds of things. Indeed, on the same day, in the same city, Maurice Smith of the *Winnipeg Free Press*, was telling the minister of National Health and Welfare (and Hockey Canada) not to be a tool in the hands of the NHL and not to let the League get away with high-handed action. In the heat of the argument it was probably overlooked that the NHL proposed no action. Be that as it may, Mr. Smith wrote: "Far better the series against the Russians be scrapped than permit the injustice the National Hockey League would perpetrate and which Hockey Canada is meekly prepared to accept." Thinking along the same lines, the *Toronto Star* editorialized that to the fans the Canada—Russia series was perhaps the biggest event in hockey history. Said the *Star*: "To the NHL, the series is obviously just a pawn to be used in its contest with the upstart World Hockey Association. It's an outrageous way to treat the home of the game." The *Star* editorialist happened to forget that to call Canada the home of hockey is historically incorrect, and in today's context (players, money and activity) a blatant falsehood. Though there was a time when Canadians played more and better hockey than anyone else.

Not surprisingly, comment in Canada's west suggested a different point of view. In the *Edmonton Journal*, which once warned editorially that the chlorination of water was

a Communist plot to weaken our resistance against the Bolsheviks, Wayne Overland refused to blame the NHL and instead directed a blast against Hockey Canada for, "promoting the interests of the NHL to the detriment of the citizens of Canada . . ."

If outrage in the name of public opinion was a media must, then Ted Blackman, the brilliant sports editor of the *Montreal Gazette*, served the call of duty best. He wrote: "Ah, the National Hockey League, it stinks. Even the players, often portrayed as the greediest animals on the face of this earth, unplugged their cash registers for two months to take part in this national affair. But the owners couldn't resist the opportunity to milk a genuine occasion of sport for another ounce of blood money." No doubt Ted Blackman wrung tears from thousands of Montreal Lakeshore commuters with that unabashed bit of early morning scorn. As the drama unfolded and the games got under way, Blackman found still stronger stuff to keep the tearducts moist. If anyone had taken the trouble to measure the emotions stirred by the Hull-abaloo on a sort of rating scale of national interests and concerns, the Hull affair would probably have been plotted near the top. The following comments by Jack Koffman in the *Ottawa Citizen* represent an inspired record of the moment. On July 14 he lamented, predicted and warned as follows: as follows:
"Everyone laughed when the name *Team Canada* was

coined for the pro All-Stars who are to oppose Russia in the long-awaited hockey series in September.

"The laughing's all over, however.

"Instead, fans across the country are boiling at the gall of the greedy, selfish, National Hockey League owners in barring Bobby Hull.

"And a giant-sized share of the anger is being directed towards that wonderful organization known as Hockey Canada. Next time medals for stupidity are handed out, Hockey Canada should be No. 1 on the hit parade for permitting the NHL to write its own rules for a show that's supposed to be national.

"But I'll bet an exception is made in Hull's case. The country's too mad.

"At the same time, don't wait for anyone to say a kind word for Doug Fisher, the former NDP member who suddenly has blossomed as a sports authority, or his Hockey Canada colleagues. Fisher is chairman of Hockey Canada's executive committee. Did he get the post because he can take orders from the NHL without argument?

"He'd like the hockey world to believe that the rule which bars the Golden Jet, along with any other pro hockey player who jumped to the WHA, is a mere coincidence at a time when the NHL monopoly is being threatened.

"Did you ever hear such rot?

"For years Canadian fans have bemoaned the fact that the Russians kept knocking off our hockey teams because we weren't allowed to use our best players. Finally, the NHL came to terms with Hockey Canada to make the pro athletes available.

"A few months ago it appeared to be a magnificent concession by the National Hockey League people. They were prepared, people believed, to disrupt their own training programs in order to give this country top representation against the boys from Moscow.

"But it doesn't turn out to be the real story. The NHL was simply taking steps to protect itself against the new league. Here was a chance, the old establishment felt, to become heroes to Canadian hockey fans and, at the same time, strike a blow against the new league.

"I'm amazed that Harry Sinden is willing to coach *Team Canada* under these circumstances.

"He's the chap who walked out on Boston Bruins almost hours after bringing the *Stanley Cup* to Boston. He didn't like the way the Bruins were operating, felt he wasn't being paid what he deserved.

"Well, surprisingly, Sinden sat in the Prime Minister's office yesterday and intimated he could get along very nicely as coach of *Team Canada* with or without Hull.

"The Prime Minister's office took a hand to convince owners of Montreal Canadiens they should back down from their stand that Forum season ticket subscribers should get first call on the Russian visit to the Forum.

"Apparently, though, Pierre Trudeau and Health Minister John Munro both feel they should not interfere with Hockey Canada's handling of *Team Canada*. Well, if the pair want to ask some of the voters for expressions of opinion, they'd soon learn most people are willing to give Hockey Canada the bounce as of this minute.

"Hull is the second highest scorer in the history of the NHL. He's the only man ever to score 50 goals or more in five different seasons. There is no adequate way of describing what the Golden Jet has meant to pro hockey.

"That's why I feel the NHL finally went too far and won't get away with it. Gouging the public repeatedly by giving them watered-down expansion hockey at inflation prices never met with the complete approval of the customers. Picking up bundles of money by charging the new clubs millions for exactly nothing brought some beefs, but it never went beyond that.

"Now, the public is about ready to go to war with the NHL magnates."

Ottawa government officials, in the meantime, had got the message to lay off or risk withdrawal, by the owners, of a dozen or so selected players in exchange for Bobby Hull's participation. That all was well and equanimity reigned in Ottawa, and particularly in Hockey Canada, did not appear to be exactly true. The sudden calm, a day after training camp opened and after Bobby Hull's no-show had become an irrevocable fact. It was surprising, considering the campaign that had been waged by so many, in such powerful quarters, with so much ferocity, to force Hull's participation.

The media, overnight and to a man, waxed delirious about the calibre of the selects, and could not have sounded more convinced and convincing about the inevitability of total disaster for the *Soviet Nationals*. So, who needed Bobby Hull?

The clearest, simplest comments on the Hull-abaloo came from two lawyers, Eagleson and Campbell. It had become apparent that not the Canadian Amateur Hockey Association, nor the Hockey Canada authorities were in command of *Team Canada*, even though the CAHA was the official sanctioning body for the series, while Hockey Canada was the official promoter, organizer and financier of *Team Canada*. The real boss was none other than Alan Eagleson, officially executive director of the NHL Players' Association, and member of the board of Hockey Canada. Having squared with Clarence Campbell, president of the NHL, Mr. Eagleson settled things by saying "Hull or 14 to 16 others," and made it stick.

As for the NHL, one of its members, Maple Leaf owner Ballard, remained silent after Mr. Campbell had firmly and precisely insisted that Hull would not play. On a television program, the NHL president said that the NHL was not going to give one inch to the newly established WHA.

"Defecting players represent a tremendous expense to the NHL," said Campbell. The expense cut two ways. Losing players to the WHA meant loss of the investment in them and possible loss of gate receipts from fans who had been paying high prices to see their favourite stars. It also meant pressure for higher salaries to match or better the offers made by the WHA. While in recent years the salaries of NHL players had gone up from averages in the mid teens to the high thirties, in 1972 salaries demanded and agreed to were at least double those in the 1970-71 season. It has been estimated that by the end of the current season, NHL owners will have paid $5 million more for player talent than they paid two years earlier.

Mr. Campbell asked the Canadian public if there was any reason why the NHL should help the WHA. "There is no reason why we should put on parade the showpiece of the other side. You don't show off the competition's best product. I don't want to predict disaster. I just hope that no course of action will be recommended that will be impossible for the people involved."

Having said that the NHL could not and would not compromise, Mr. Campbell made light of public and political pressure. "The NHL governors," said Campbell, "will not change their minds because of an emotional response. Some of them think that the response is one of ingratitude. They feel that the NHL has supported hockey in Canada by providing players for the series and by contributing financially to minor hockey for years and years. So far, all we have received in return is abuse. The star players of NHL teams will be playing 30 days more than in any other season, and we worry about their condition at the end of the season. We also worry about the risk of injury and the loss of the players for the NHL exhibition schedule. The NHL players on *Team Canada* represent $2.5 million in salaries . . . and all we have received is abuse."

So much for Clarence Campbell. He had his point, no doubt legally correct, and stated it with admirable cool. Eagleson did not dispute the matter but let it be known to his friends that it could have been settled in Hull's and *Team Canada's* favour, had Bobby been a little more pliant and had he shown up at a meeting in the Chicago office of his one-time employers, the Black Hawks.

Hull was seen briefly in the *Team Canada* training camp. Campbell and Eagleson were very much in evidence, often together, in the first days of the camp in Toronto. They went about their business (and our business) unrepentant, unprotected and unmolested. No one caught second wind to let them have it; they were not going to let Canada have Bobby. No one opened the files on the NHL to figure out why precisely the American owners should expect our gratitude; or for that matter, why and how the NHL could prevent the Canadian government from having three dozen Canadian citizens of Canada's choice serve a non-commercial purpose with potential financial benefits only to the NHL. So it looked as if we should have shown unequivocal gratitude to the NHL for allowing us the use of its darlings, in the custody of Mr. Eagleson, under the banner of Canada.

Out of the affair emerged two heroes. Bobby, a few millions the richer, leaving Canadians with the "we'll-never-know" illusion that with Hull on the team things would not have been as tough as they turned out to be. Bobby's reputation remains intact and his loyalties to hockey above suspicion. The other hero—Alan Eagleson, authentic Canadian Godfather who fixed it all with offers that no one refused. Whatever his offers were and by what right he made them, has been lost sight of. Only the Russians kept wondering . . . suspicious lot that they are.

Phil Esposito, Paul Henderson, say, "Thank you, Bobby Hull." Canadians, Hockey Canada, Clarence Campbell, NHL governors, everybody, say, "Thank you, Alan Eagleson."

With Bobby Hull the victory might have been even sweeter . . . Without Eagleson there might have been no contest at all. . . .

We'll never know.

H.W.H.

Eagleson — The Boss

Just for a few seconds there, you could hear it in their voices, which suddenly grew careful, measured. Alan Eagleson, who at the moment is the most powerful man in hockey, was sitting in the VIP lounge at Montreal Airport, running through a few housekeeping details between planes with Patrick Reid, the man from External Affairs who, for the past few months, has been working full-time on arrangements for the historic Canada — Soviet hockey series.

It was a brisk and amiable little meeting, with papers spread out all over the coffee table and free drinks arriving repeatedly from the VIP bar, as the two men worked quickly to dispatch some outstanding details: Whom do we send to Prague as advance man for *Team Canada's* games against the Czechs after the Soviet series is over? What colour jerseys will they wear? And what about the air-freight charges on all that Canada Packers meat and Labatt's beer and Canada Dry soda water being flown to Moscow? Who's going to pay for that?

Until that moment, it was two minds running along parallel tracks. Now, suddenly, the vibes had changed. We're in a conflict situation now, and Eagleson says carefully:

"Well, I thought the government would be picking up that part of the tab."

Reid, an elegant Irishman, puts a little civilized muscle in his voice. He explains that, in his view, the government is already paying for a hell of a lot of things it didn't imagine it would end up paying for, and . . .

Eagleson backtracks, gracefully. "We'll settle it later," he says. "We'll talk to Air Canada and get back to you." Instantly, the mood relaxes, and the two men move on to details that don't involve bargaining, such as who in the Hockey Canada delegation should get VIP treatment from our embassy in Moscow.

I don't want to overstress that incident. Really, it was nothing — just a flash of inconclusive haggling, involving perhaps $3,000, in a huge international deal that has involved literally thousands of such details. I'm reporting it because, for me, it symbolizes the real fascination of this series — the fact that, when those two teams face each other in the Forum tomorrow night, their presence on the same sheet of ice is the result of a miracle of compromise by dozens of opposing interests — everything from the opposing social systems of Canada and the Soviet Union to the conflicting aims of all the overlapping bureaucracies that constitute organized hockey; to the large companies and their ad agencies that are paying up to $27,500 a minute for TV time; to the politicians who are jockeying for whatever political advantage they can extract from the event.

Each one of those thousands of small compromises, moreover, involved some kind of a human confrontation — some moment when two men looked into each other's eyes and read that old, primal message: We're on opposite sides now, and only one of us is going to win.

Conflict is the most fundamental rule of life. Duality, yin-yang, dialectics, good-versus-evil, call it what you like — but always there is this struggle against some kind of opposing force, either inside or outside yourself. Conflict is how men become saints, how infants learn to walk, how nations govern themselves, how all organizations function, how amoebas evolve, how people grow. Nothing could be more primal, and that is why this hockey series will engage the attention of millions of people and create a cash-flow of tens of millions of dollars. Hockey, for Canadians and for Russians, is one of the great allegories of the kind of people we are, and what we think about life.

It is a kind of existential ballet, a celebration of the conflict that makes life grow. So it's only natural that the greatest series in the history of the game should have been arranged by the kind of men for whom conflict and its resolution is a process as familiar as breathing.

Eagleson, is one of those men, perhaps the most accomplished conflict-manager in organized hockey. He sprints through life like a million-dollar insurance salesman, spinning off roughly a deal a minute, reconciling human opposites the way a computer works with binary numbers.

He walks down airport corridors at a speed which, for most men, would be a fast jog. He's the kind of man who sits tensely poised, his fingers drumming anxiously against the vinyl upholstery, for the 15-second interval it takes a cab-driver to fill out a receipt.

Then he dashes into the lobby of Sutton Place, where he's keeping a suite for the duration of the Canadian series, and makes at least three decisions before he reaches the elevator. The doorman wants a pennant autographed. Done! Some junior hockey type, who's been waiting for Eagleson in the lobby, steps forward in supplication. Gotcha! Somebody else approaches him about tickets. No sweat! In his slim briefcase, you see, he carries a king's ransom worth of series tickets. As he races through his day he dispenses them to doormen and corporation presidents— always at $15 the pair—like a medieval bishop dispensing indulgences.

Eagleson may be the ultimate Toronto influence-broker. He is president of the Ontario Progressive Conservatives, president of the National Hockey League Players' Association, a director of Hockey Canada, partner in the largest "young" law firm in the country—and so he is the

Mr. Connection who stands at the vertices of all kinds of overlapping establishments.

Somebody need a hockey rink? Al will call his friend Harold Ballard, president of Maple Leaf Gardens, and the thing is done. Some hospital needs money? Al will call his pal at Molson's or Ford or the Toronto-Dominion Bank and the thing is done. Somebody's kid is dying to see Monday's game at the Gardens? No problem, Al can arrange it. At a cocktail party on Wednesday afternoon, I saw him sell $25,000 worth of TV time before he'd finished his first highball.

There are a number of people in this town—Eddie Goodman, for instance, or Robert Macaulay, or Keith Davey—who owe their livelihoods to the fact that they can pick up the phone any time and get through to a bank president or a cabinet minister or a newspaper publisher and settle large matters in five minutes flat, including three minutes of chummy banter about hockey. But nobody is better at this game than Alan Eagleson.

He knows that power depends on access, and he knows that access is based on trust. The people who trust him include Bill Davis, who is premier of Ontario, and Bobby Orr, the greatest hockey player in history. Much of Eagleson's power stems from his relationship with these two men, and it makes for a weird and potent connection between hockey and politics.

"To me," says Eagleson, "hockey *is* politics. It's what I enjoy. The only difference is that, on one side I'm representing 'management'—the Conservative government—and on the other I'm representing 'labor,' the National Hockey League (NHL) players.

"It's all a matter of lobbying, of convincing people they can trust you, of knowing what you're talking about. Sure I've got power. I could blow the whistle at 8:15 on Saturday night, and there'd be no game against the Russians. As I told them in Russia once: 'Sure the NHL owns the teams. But wouldn't it look kind of funny with Clarence Campbell playing centre? But the more power you have, the less you need to use it.'

In the five years since Eagleson formed the Players' Association, the average salaries of NHL players have risen from about $15,000 to the $40,000 neighborhood. He represents 150 of the league's 320 players, and most of the rest will do what he suggests. Which is why Eagleson, throughout the infinitely tricky negotiations that led up to the series, held a virtual veto power on everything that transpired.

Hockey Canada is the organization set up by the federal government to upgrade the amateur aspect of the game, and to represent Canada's efforts in international competition. But it wasn't Hockey Canada that conducted the most crucial negotiations with the Russians, and Eagleson now cheerfully admits that he's spent much of the past few months "un-negotiating" much of what was painstakingly negotiated with the Russians by other segments of Canadian hockey's multicellular bureaucracy.

Eagleson, along with a lot of other people, has been working towards Saturday's confrontation since 1969. To do so involved resolution of a gigantic conflict: Canadians are the best hockey players in the world, but most of them work for American capitalists, and the czars of international hockey insist that world hockey is an amateur activity. Which meant that, all through the 1950s and 1960s, Canadian amateurs, who made their livings in filling stations and sausage factories were losing too many games against "amateurs" from Czechoslovakia and Sweden and the Soviet Union who made their living playing hockey for the state.

In 1970, in Hockey Canada's first major decision, we withdrew from international competition, including the Olympics, until these rules could be changed.

Before and after this decision, the Russians were making conciliatory noises. They wanted to learn, they said, and they wanted their teams to play against the best. But how could it be arranged? Certain hints were dropped.

These approaches had a quasi-diplomatic character—like sending Chester Ronning on tippy-toe to Hanoi—and Eagleson initiated at least one of them. In 1969, during a tournament in Sweden, he tried to approach the Russians. Three times they declined to see him, he says. Then, flying to Moscow, he announced that he "represented the workers of the NHL". In short order he met with Russia's top-ranking hockey officials, but the results were inconclusive—perhaps because Eagleson, from the Soviet point of view, represented no one but himself.

The breakthrough didn't come until last March, when Canada sent a three-man negotiating team to Prague, hoping to work out some new rules that would permit "open" competition—any Canadian would be eligible for a Canadian team, in other words, regardless of his professional status. But the Russians declined to sit down with Charlie Hay, Hockey Canada's representative on the committee, or with Lou Lefaive, who was there to represent the federal government. The only man they'd talk to was the third member of the negotiating team, a Calgary lawyer named Joe Kryczka who is president of the Canadian Amateur Hockey Association.

They met at the International Hotel, a stone-and-concrete Stalinist horror on the outskirts of Prague which, it is rumored, was originally designed as an officers' barracks or a political prison. Kryczka and Gordon Juckes, another CAHA official, sat down at a small table in an upstairs room with an interpreter named Victor and Andre Starovoitov, secretary of the Soviet Hockey Federation.

The Russian message was stunning: they were finally

ready to play Canada's best, despite their fears of jeopardizing their amateur status in Olympic competition.

From there on, for two solid weeks in that musty little cell of a room, the four men haggled over the details.

Finally it was settled: A Canadian team would play the Russians in September, four games in Canada, four in the Soviet Union. Eagleson flew over on two days' notice to lay down his assurances that the NHL players, his clients, would be available to play.

This turned out to be news to the owners of the teams in the NHL, all of whom are unsentimental capitalists, and all but two of whom are unsentimental American capitalists. Many couldn't see why such expensive, and such terrifyingly perishable assets as their hockey players should be deployed in a physically risky contest against the Russians.

The match could have foundered on this issue alone, but Eagleson, Irish ward-heeler that he is, found a way to bring the owners into line.

"I spoke the only language they understand," he says. "Money."

Eagleson, at that point, was in the middle of a lengthy haggling session with the NHL over players' pensions. Using this as leverage, he put together a deal whereby part of the profits from the series would be paid into the players' pension fund. This not only saved the owners money—since it reduced the amount Eagleson would demand from them—it also gave the player a long-term financial incentive.

In addition to this carrot, Eagleson wielded a stick: If the NHL wouldn't co-operate, he told the papers, he'd send "the Al Eagleson All-Stars" to Russia, meaning his own friends and clients, playing for Canada on his say-so, regardless of the NHL's wishes.

The deal could have foundered again when, as every literate Canadian is now aware, it turned out that Bobby Hull was ineligible for *Team Canada* because he'd signed with a rival league, the fledgling World Hockey Association.

Do we need to recapitulate this squalid episode in the story of our diminishing nationhood? It caused far more public outcry than, say, the King-Byng constitutional crisis of 1926 and it was ably summed up in a *Star* editorial:

"The sad fact is that we sold our national game, and now have to beg and borrow to get star players to represent Canada."

Precisely. If hockey is a Canadian allegory, one of its more grisly parallels is the fact that our national sport, like our natural resources, has become a branch-office outpost of American megabusiness.

Eagleson, in haggling with the owners, had evolved an understanding that to be eligible for *Team Canada*, a player must have signed with the NHL. "It was designed as a protection for both players and owners," he says.

Interestingly, this understanding was never spelled out in a written agreement that could be produced in court. But Eagleson knows his power rests on other people's trust, even hockey-club owners, and so he stuck to his word.

Despite petitions, billboards, hot-line harangues, the telegraphed intervention of Pierre Trudeau and furtive attempts at conciliation by Health Minister John Munro, the deal stayed firm and Bobby Hull stayed home.

"Who's Bobby Hull?" Eagleson says now. "Everybody's forgotten about it. Today's news is tomorrow's garbage."

By this point, you may have noticed that Eagleson is having much more say in managing this deal than is Hockey Canada, the agency set up by Ottawa to do that very thing. That is embarrassingly true, and a number of Hockey Canada's highly-paid officials are displeased about it. They are a formidable crew of bluesuits, schooled in the mysteries of systems analysis and the Harvard case method, exponents of corporate liberalism in a world of 19th-century buccaneers. So it's not surprising that Eagleson, with his flair for Tammany Hall trade-offs, seems more effective at getting things done.

Take television, a subject about which Eagleson proudly proclaims his ignorance. It seemed only natural, by *droit de seigneur* almost, that Maclaren Advertising, which has produced Hockey Night in Canada since time immemorial, should get the TV rights to the greatest sporting event since man learned to skate. Last June the agency announced it would acquire these rights for $500,000, a piece of news which Eagleson received with great dismay.

He raised hell at Hockey Canada. He did more. With a few magical phone calls, he put together TC Productions Limited, a company owned by Garden's owner Ballard, and his 23-year-old client Bobby Orr. TC offered $750,000 for the radio and TV rights. It was a non-profit deal for everyone but the cause of hockey, since Eagleson proposed to turn over the first $200,000 of any profits to Hockey Canada, the next $50,000 to the CAHA. All profits beyond that would be split between Hockey Canada and the NHL players' pension fund. After giving Maclaren and any other agencies a few days to outbid TC's offer, Eagleson found himself, an utter amateur, presiding over the biggest television deal in Canadian history.

It is instructive to hear him tell how he sold the ads that will punctuate those 176 minutes, which will be shared with an audience estimated at eight million: "I sold roughly $2.2 million worth of advertising very, very quickly," he says, "and I did it by calling my friends.

"I called Peter Hardy at Labatt's, and he was in for $800,000. Earl Brownridge at CCM came in for $200,000. My friend Bill Bremner from Vickers & Benson sold Ford for $600,000. And Art Harnett brought in Edge Shaving Cream for $110,000. Hell, even the radio rights did well.

Hockey Canada's original price was $40,000. Well, we asked $120,000. We didn't get it, but at least it got people thinking about the right kind of figures. We've got $80,000 so far, and all the time isn't sold yet."

Eagleson made one mistake: He didn't know about the 15 per cent commission that ad agencies customarily charge their clients. He discovered to his horror that TC would be netting $325,000 less from the deal than he's calculated. Once again, he got on the telephone, appealing to the sponsors and their agencies to trim the commissions, just this once, in the interests of patriotism and hockey. Most agreed, but the sponsors with the most clout, Labatt's and Toronto-Dominion Bank, proposed binding arbitration. The impartial arbitrator they wanted, moreover, was on Labatt's own board of directors—incredible effrontery, except that the man was Eddie Goodman, lawyer, political fixer, power broker.

Everybody trusts Eddie Goodman, including Eagleson. And so the session took place earlier this week in Goodman's office, and the upshot was a Solomon-like judgment that satisfied everyone, more or less. The agencies may receive much less than they thought they were getting, but they'll have a chance to feel patriotic. Besides, all these men will be making deals with each other for years to come. And favors once granted are never forgotten.

"This seems to be the year for writing million-dollar cheques," he says. "Bobby Hull got one. Well, I'm going to have Bobby Orr write one—a million bucks for hockey, the profit from that TV deal."

Eagleson is now wearing so many hats that when he catches a plane, which is more or less constantly these days, he has to stop and figure out which outfit to bill the ticket to. Some of his less fervent admirers have accused him of conflict of interest. After one such suggestion from a Hockey Canada director, Eagleson tendered his resignation —something he does fairly routinely. It was, of course, not accepted.

What's his angle? I hear people saying. "What's his cut?" Well, to suppose that Eagleson is motivated by anything so sordid as money is to misjudge the man utterly. In an almost obsessive way, he wants the power to shape events, and he covets the access that makes such power possible. Eagleson's whole strategy in life, politics and hockey is always to be in a position to pick up the telephone, dial the private number of a premier, a bank chairman, a club owner, a superstar, a prime minister even, and say: "Hi pal—look, there's this little problem. . . ." Favors are his currency, and at the moment he's in a better position than almost anyone else in town to bestow them.

Or withhold them. One of the sweet rewards of being in unchallenged control of the television time, and the NHL players who will occupy it, is that he can shaft the Liberals.

You wouldn't believe the squalid manoeuvering that's been perpetrated by various politicians in an attempt to associate themselves with the glory of *Team Canada*. Incredible!—Like a bunch of schoolboys trying to squirm their way into the front row when the photographer comes around to take the class picture.

"Trudeau gets to drop the puck in Montreal, because that's the opening game," says Eagleson the TV czar. "Well that's okay. But would you believe he wants to drop the puck in Toronto, too, on Monday night?

"I say my friend the premier should drop the puck. Then Ottawa starts talking protocol. It's protocol, see, that a provincial premier can't drop the puck when the Prime Minister is in attendance.

"I figure, it's my television time, they're my players, I can have Joe Schlunk drop the puck if I want to. We'll see about that one.

"Also, we've made a ruling: no half-time interviews with politicians, except for one with the Prime Minister. And not even that if he calls an election!" Eagleson cackles, and his glee is exquisite to behold.

The Prime Minister's party will be sitting behind the *Team Canada* bench, and his aides no doubt imagine that eight million viewers will see him, beaming and Buddha-like, casting his radiance upon the team below. Eagleson has other ideas.

"The way I've planned it right now," he says, "is that the Prime Minister's party will be seated a little bit off to one side—do you see? But there are six great seats right above the bench where the camera's got to pan every time there's a penalty. And who's going to be in those seats? Me and my wife. Bill Davis and his wife. And Bob Stanfield and his wife, that's who!" Eagleson cackles again, marvelling at his own monstrous subtlety.

You see? The whole thing is conflict, from beginning to end. But the glory of sport, and of all civilized behavior, is that it can channel the innate aggressiveness of the human animal in healthy directions. Aggression can destroy us, or it can take us to the stars, depending on the rules we make and how well we play by them. The current series, a contest between similar young men from territories that have equipped themselves to evaporate each other, is a small step away from the trenches and toward the stars.

Alexander Ross, The Toronto Star

TEAM
CANADA

Leaving it to Harry...

Narcissus, a mythological youth, often admired his image reflected in clear pools of water. "I am beautiful and good", he said. Eventually he turned into a flower.

An American political candidate in a simpler age than ours, having little in his mind and a carefree way about him, campaigned by deriding his opponent who was a man of purpose and considerable erudition. "He reads books and things," the candidate sneered, "readin' ruins the shootin' act." His opponent shot him dead.

The Soviets put Sputnik in orbit, thus starting the race to the moon. Their achievement provoked the most extensive changes ever undertaken in American education.

"Little Cindy-Lou Who" was fooled by the Grinch because, being "not more than two," she was innocent and ignorant.

This goes to show that, unless you want to be a flower child, a dead politician, last on the moon, or have your goodies swiped, you don't take yourself too seriously, you do not underestimate the other fellow's abilities, you keep ahead of rivals in everything, and you get to know the world's Grinches.

Canadians, it seems, took their hockey too lightly before Game One and themselves too seriously after Game Four in Vancouver when beating the Russians at our own game turned out to be less of a cinch than we had imagined. Suddenly we were playing "the hockey series of the century."

Generally, the attitudes in Canada before the series betrayed over-confidence, smugness, arrogance, innocence, and a psychology as profound as a frying pan. "It's our game. They did not invent hockey. We'll show the Ruskies." That's what we said and what most Canadians believed. There were a few dissenting voices but one either ignored them or discounted them.

By chance Harry Sinden was available and possessed credentials that suited him for the job of coaching and managing *Team Canada*. By chance, and in an administrative vacuum, Alan Eagleson surfaced with the power to put the team together. In comparison, our amateurs, preparing for the Munich Olympics and usually criticised for organizing their affairs like a temperance drive in a logging camp, worked hard and long and never underrated the odds against winning medals.

Speaking for himself and for assistant coach, John Ferguson, Harry Sinden justified his choice of *Team Canada* players. He said, in part, "You have to have youth. The enthusiasm, the innocence of youth is so vital to a team that sometimes you go with lesser talent . . ." He announced his selection on July 12, said training camp would begin about three weeks before the first game, and departed with Ferguson for a scouting trip to the Soviet Union. From Moscow, some time later, he returned with these conclusions:

". . . no matter how many practice games we watch, or films we analyze, or people we talk to, it's all going to be only two per cent of the real thing. We're both going to start finding out about the 98 per cent when we hit that ice together for the first time.

"If I have a philosophy of hockey, it is that it's the game above all others where you have to stand up and be counted right from the start. You can't run out of bounds — the boards stop that. Your manliness, your guts are always on the line for all to see, and if you try to avoid some play or situation because you don't like the look of it, you've had it. I've been away from hockey for two years and I've missed it, no doubt about that. Maybe it's to my advantage: where to other coaches, the series might be one more chore — and in the middle of summer, too — to me it's a revival.

"All I know for sure is that I don't want us to do *anything* the Russians do. If they like getting up at 8 a.m., let them. We'll get up at 8.30. Actually, they usually get their players up at 6 a.m. and make them run round the hotel they're staying in. If I know anything about some Canadian pro players, they might be coming *in* at that time.

"And all I can tell you about our strategy is that we're gearing to win the first game. We'll think about the second after we've won the first. But I'll also tell you that I have complete confidence in the ability of our team to beat *any* combination of hockey players, *any* time, *any* place in the world."

When training camp convened, Sinden, Eagleson, Ferguson and Harold Ballard (who played host as owner of Maple Leaf Gardens) ran their show like a boisterous old boys' reunion, with a formal agenda conducted in the Gardens twice each day, and festivities interspersed among the remaining hours at a swank Toronto hotel competently devoted to making certain that a good time was had by all.

Two seasons earlier, Sinden had coached the Boston Bruins to victory in the NHL. He had himself played against Soviet teams in 1958 and 1960. On both occasions the Canadian teams had triumphed over the Russians. Sinden's choice of Ferguson, a former NHL player noted as much for his penalty record as for his scoring ability, had caused some consternation. "This isn't world war three," one journalist had remarked. Sinden's reply: "John was available and willing. He has this great winning spirit, loves to fight . . . hates to lose . . . He was my first choice."

Sinden had to contend with conflicting authorities, loose discipline, confidence over-kill, and utter disregard for what the Russians might have up their sleeves. "Leave it to Harry," everybody said. But there was some doubt that Harry Sinden was in control. "There are things you cannot expect from people who are stars and who make great sacrifices to play for their country . . ." Sinden was heard to say.

The Canadian coaches accepted a nonchalant buddy relationship with their players. In contrast, coaches Bobrov and Kulagin, both of them commissioned officers in the Soviet armed forces, appeared to demand and get respect and unquestioning obedience from their players. Unlike *Team Canada*, the *USSR Nationals* and their coaches also appeared to be sensitive to what they termed "public opinion" and to the impressions that they made on and off the ice. It was naïve and unprofessional on the part of *Team Canada* and Hockey Canada to ignore both the Russians and the Canadian public and to leave things to Harry . . .

And to Harry we had left it . . . all of the legend, the symbols, the mythology . . .

Dick Beddoes of the Toronto *Globe and Mail* described the risks in an article entitled, "Only a game, but 15 million fans want fame, not shame." He wrote:

It is only a game that small boys play, in South Porcupine and Sheep Tracks and Moscow and Minsk, six kids to a side and keep your head up.

Only a game, often vivid and reckless, the one sport where Canadians can put a poultice on wounded vanities by being good at something the Americans aren't good at. If Canada cares about supremacy in anything it is hockey and, dammit, shoot that puck.

But a small nagging thought intrudes on the morning of the first game of a summit series. No matter how big the game, the fate of civilization will turn on extraneous events and several hundred million Chinese will remain unaware of the final score.

Only a game, but don't bother 15-million Canadians with reminders that this is merely child's play. This is our game, baby, and our best must preserve it from the grasping maulies of hairy-legged furriners.

Foster Hewitt will grab that many Canadians by the throat of their attention when his staccato voice leaps out of their television sets at 8 p.m. . . . . "Hello Canada, and hockey fans in Siberia and Omsk!"

Only a game that begins at 3 o'clock tomorrow morning in Moscow, but as many as 100-million Russians may be exposed to the picture of padded big kids spoiling for a fight in the Montreal Forum.

One Moscow viewer will be Mrs. Vera Petrovaka Tretiak, a middle-aged woman who played bandy on frozen ponds with a curved stick and small rubber ball. When her son, Vladislav, was 11, she put a hockey stick in his hand and here he is, nine years later, the best goaltender in the Soviet Union. Maybe he marches to the same drummer as those resolute chaps who went for the downs in irrational streams of blood at Stalingrad, in 1942.

Only a game, but one of the newest brides in Moscow might tell you to stick such a suggestion in your old babooshka. Her name is Mrs. Tatiana Tretiak, married exactly nine days ago to the Soviet goalkeeper. A story, as Boris Pasternak might have said, goes with it.

On Aug. 22, on the eve of his wedding, Vladislav Tretiak was beaten for eight goals in a game in Moscow.

Later he was approached by Viktor Khotorhkin, the tall official interpreter of the Soviet nationals.

"Eight goals," Khotorhkin said in mock amazement. "What happened, Vlad?"

A fugitive smile touched briefly on Tretiak's young, unmarked expression, which resembles the high-cheekboned features of an immature Stan Mikita.

"Ah, Viktor," Tretiak said. "With Tatania on my mind, I'm thinking about something else besides hockey."

Only a game, but don't try to talk about anything else tonight in the beer rooms of Flin Flon and the sleazy bars in Sudbury and the Esposito household in Sault Ste. Marie.

Look, it's like this in Canadian hockey. Schmautzie's father, let us say, never got out of the coal mine, so Schmautzie must perform one of those second generation arabesques that makes Canada, in hockey, the land of the rising son.

Few sons of any Canadian family have risen higher in hockey than Phil and Tony Esposito and here they were yesterday, prominent and vocal in a brisk practice obviously intended to psyche the Soviet witnesses.

"Watch out, Popsy!" yelled big Phil as he drove a puck at Ed Johnston, the Boston goaler who at the advanced age of 36, is called Pops by his playmates. Oh, to be 36 again (this is a small boy at the typewriter) and picked to play in this series.

The vintage Russian, 31-year-old Rags Ragulin, watched as the Canadians exhibited major grace, passion and invention and a little hot dog. "They skate better than we do," Ragulin said.

Only a game, but even the most cerebral of players is hooked on its momentary importance. "If standing up for the national anthems tonight doesn't grab us," says Ken Dryden, "nothing will."

Dryden is a sophisticate aware of a world beyond the playpen, concerned enough about the way we have raped the planet to spend last summer working in Washington for Ralph Nader, the consumer watchdog.

But Dryden was in goal for the old *Team Canada* one night in Vancouver in December, 1969, when the *Russian Nationals* pumped nine goals past him in a 9-3 romp. He will be in goal tonight and he has a lot to pay them back for.

Only a game, but don't act casually about it if you are around Grant Warwick, wherever he is. Warwick coached Penticton Vees to a frantic 5-0 conquest of the Russians in the 1955 world tournament in Krefeld, Germany.

Afterward Warwick sounded as though all his glands were misfiring. "Thank God we beat them!" he said.

Only a game, and this one has Canadians in a pressure cooker. Although in children's games, I believe, God is neutral.

To which Ted Blackman of *The Montreal Gazette* did not reply, "Amen." Blackman must have lumped divine partiality, his own and everybody else's into one conclusion, when he wrote:

No matter how slick Bobrov and his Bobcats look in practice, they have never faced a team from this country that is prepared so well and staffed so fully. They'll meet a dozen Carl Brewers tonight.

Brewer, you'll remember, had the Russians mesmerized back in 1967. His play helped Canada beat Russia in the Centennial Tournament and, but for an injury, he would have given us the world championship that year. Well, Brad Park is better than Carl Brewer and he has Phil Esposito with him, not Gary Dineen; Yvan Cournoyer, not Fran Huck.

The best Russia can hope to do is steal a game on hot goaltending, cold officiating or our own over-confidence. More likely, Bobrov's Bobcats will be Pavlov's Kittens by the time this junket reaches the west coast. It'll be 5-1 tonight for Canada, the start of the eight-game sweep.

Remember, if I'm right, you read it here first.

Yes, one remembers, but one would like to forget. "Over-confidence" did cross Ted Blackman's mind, be it ever so fleetingly . . .

In another Montreal paper, *The Star*, John Robertson examined our mood and mind mid-way through *Team Canada's* training camp:

The stories you read out of the Canadian training camp report patriotic fervor at a high pitch. The athletes are being resoundingly applauded for giving up part of their summer to play for their country. If this doesn't give them a sense of well being, they are being told every time they pick up a newspaper or turn on a radio that they are beyond doubt the greatest hockey machine ever assembled, and that the Russians will be lucky to stay within three or four goals of them. They are being driven reasonably hard by a very competent coach, but it seems there's almost too much camaraderie, too much mutual admiration and absolutely no fear of being out from the squad if they don't perform up to scratch.

The Russians, on the other hand, have several advantages in this area. First, as underdogs, nobody is telling them that the NHLers will be easy meat. On the contrary, they are likely being brainwashed daily with the edict that nothing less than optimum performance will win for them. While the Canadians frankly expect to win, the Russians will be taking nothing for granted. This will be especially evident in their training camp in progress now.

Keeping a sense of perspective on his, the optimistic, side of the balance, Red Fisher, followed Robertson's train of thought in a *Montreal Star* column, ten days later.

Esposito is walking along a Toronto street. The first intra-squad game is only a few days away (his team lost, but Esposito scored twice and assisted on another) and he's saying:

"I've never felt better. I really feel good. I mean . . . I've been in Harry's camps before. My brother Tony says it's the toughest camp he's ever been in, but I like it. And Harry . . . he made me feel pretty good by naming me one of the co-captains. He made me feel real good."

"Harry says you can be the leader on this team."

"That so? Did Harry say that?" asked Esposito. "That's good. That's great."

It's eight days ago, and *Team Canada* is scrimmaging, as it has been doing on most mornings. There was a bonus awaiting the players that day. Only one practice. The boredom was starting to creep in, and that's why there was only one practice scheduled.

Bill Goldsworthy has the puck and Jean Ratelle moves in to check him. It's been done thousands of times before without any mishap. This time, Ratelle tries to lift Goldsworthy's stick with his own — and misses. The stick bites into the flesh at the corner of Goldsworthy's right eye, scrapes across the eyeball, leaving a few woodchips, and then thunks into Goldsworthy's nose. The nose looks broken. The pain in the eye is excruciating, but nobody suspects it, because Goldsworthy turns, brushes at a rivulet of blood running down his cheek and goes to the dressing room.

Later, Goldsworthy has a patch fitted onto his injured eye. Coach Ferguson calls him on the telephone.

"How's the eye?" he asks.

"Ah . . . the doc put a patch on it," says Goldsworthy, "but it's okay. Lookit, about that game tomorrow night, there's nothing wrong with my legs. Get me a mask and I'll play. I want to play."

"Can you imagine that?" Ferguson was to mention later, "a patch on one eye, and he wants to play." Ferguson shook his head in wonderment, "What can you say about these guys?"

What is there to say about this *Team Canada*? It was spawned in turmoil and controversy, but since the small irritations were removed and/or settled, it has become the finest professional hockey team ever assembled. The key word is TEAM. They are more than a group of All-Stars. A fusion has taken place during the last weeks that makes this much more than a gathering of super talents. It is more than a passle of strangers thrown together for flag and country. It is not a team of All-Stars. It is an All-Star TEAM!

Since this is so, is there any reason to believe that there is something great to fear in terms of winning and losing from the athletes *Team Canada* meets tonight in the first of eight games in Canada and Moscow?

At one time, there may have been. Not any more.

Scratch any of the people associated with this noble venture, and you'll probably find that one of their great fears was the attitude the players would bring into camp. Small irritations? Big complaints? A feeling that they were whisked out of the comfort of a summer layoff or removed from the rewards of hockey schools? If the players had come into camp with their irritations and complaints, that would have hurt. None did. If any of them are unhappy, it hasn't been evident. The opposite has been true.

What, then, awaits *Team Canada* tonight and in the games to follow? Is *Team Canada* likely to overwhelm the Soviets? Eight games? Seven? A tight series?

Early in this *Team Canada* exercise, the question was put to Boris Kulagin, a florid-faced man who is the No. 2 coach of the *Soviet Nationals*.

"All that a coach can do," he said, "is to think about winning, because it is important for the team to think of winning. If the coach does not think that way, the team will not think that way. I would not like to say how many games the Soviets will win or lose, because the games will tell. But I have heard in many places that the Canadians expect to win eight games. That, I assure you, will not happen."

Perhaps.

If the Soviets have one thing going for them, it surely is in the area of conditioning. *Team Canada* goes into the series tonight without really knowing how far ahead in conditioning the Soviets are, but one thing is certain: they are. But how do they do in raw talent? Is there a Yvan Cournoyer or a Frank Mahovlich or a Brad Park on this team? Is there a Ken Dryden or a Tony Esposito among the goaltenders?

John McLellan, who is the coach of the Toronto Maple Leafs, and who was sent to Russia along with Bob Davidson to scout the Soviets at work, sits in a small room and considers the question. He fidgets. He looks at *Team Canada* coach Sinden and smiles thinly.

"It's a good question," he finally says. "If you're asking me how many of the players I saw can earn a place on *Team Canada*, I'd say one . . . I think!"

The Soviets have the conditioning but *Team Canada* isn't short on it.

Team Canada has the shooters. It has the goaltending. Is

there more? Dedication, perhaps? *Team Canada* players don't carry it on their sleeves, but it's there. Ask any of the players who aren't in the lineup tonight how much they wanted to play, and you'll know that it's there. Ask any of the players who are playing tonight!

Almost three weeks of training . . . many months of planning. Turmoil. Controversy. Arguments. Hard work. and now it's here . . . tonight.

I don't think *Team Canada* will lose a game.

That was one prediction on opening night, September 2, a few hours before Game One. Fisher had been with the training camp for nearly three weeks. His heart and his mind told him what we all wanted to hear. But he had noted and reported some symptoms of doubt and imperfection from which his colleague Robertson drew the pessimist's conclusions . . . the Soviets would win six out of eight games. Robertson's prediction earned him an invitation on a national television program, a few hours before the first game, as "the only s.o.b. among the media people."

Among the French Canadian press, there was a lonely dissenter as well. Michel Blanchard, sole among nine *La Presse* writers, not only reasoned like Robertson, he predicted in his paper's September 2 edition ". . . possible defeat for *Team Canada*, certainly no eight-game sweep, and the likeliest outcome of all: 4-3-1 for *Team Canada*." Given the mood of Montrealers, Blanchard's courage was as great as his prediction proved accurate.

For the record, there is a list of cognoscenti who were polled in Montreal before the game started. This is what they said:

Al Cauley, CJAD Sports Director: "Russia might win two, but I don't think they'll win any."

Brian MacFarlane, Hockey Night in Canada: "6-2 for Canada."

Jacques Plante, Toronto goalie: "Eight straight for Canada."

Jerry Eskenazi, *New York Times*: "The NHL team will slaughter them in eight straight."

Milt Dunnell, *Toronto Star*: Canada will win handily; they might lose one in Moscow. Say 7-1.

Claude Larochelle, Sports Editor, *Le Soleil* of Quebec City: "We may lose one in Russia. 7-1 for Canada."

Foster Hewitt, play-by-play telecaster: "Canada's two goals a game better. It looks like 8-0 Canada."

Dick Beddoes, *Toronto Globe and Mail*: "Canada to romp in eight — it's a Russian team in decay."

Fran Rosa, *Boston Globe*: "8-0 Canada — and that's also the score of the first game."

Mark Mulvoy, *Sports Illustrated*: "Canada, 7-1."

Glenn Cole, *Canadian Press*: "The Russians will win at least two games, both probably back in Russia."

Red Storey, Former NHL referee: "Canada in eight straight — but the toughest win will be the opener."

Jim Coleman: *Southam News Services*: Canada will win seven, with one game tied on Russian ice."

Anatoly Davidenko, chief economist, Soviet trade delegation to Canada: "Russia four, Canada four-friendship."

Johnny Esaw, sports director, CTV network: "The Russians will win one here, one in Russia."

Dave Bell, former CKVL and CKAC radio personality (now with Montreal's Quebec Jr. A League team): "Eight straight for Canada."

Claude Mouton, Forum and Jarry Park announcer: "six to two for Canada."

Brian Conacher, color man on telecast: Canada, 6-2.

Jim Fanning, Expos' general manager: "Three to one for Canada here, two apiece in Russia."

And so *Team Canada* "faced the music" of Game One, with the sound of Bobby Orr's groupies, the Boston Gibson Girls, still ringing in their ears" . . . Canada is the best this year, the best year, the best this year . . . the very, very best . . . we love *Team Canada*, oh yes we do . . . we're the Gibson Girls and we love you . . ."

It wasn't exactly a Greek chorus in classic tradition. But then, neither was the Canadian Narcissus contemplating his reflection in clear water.

H.W.H.

Three Dozen Super Stars

Team Canada is probably the best hockey team in the game's history. The depth of players with a complete repertoire of hockey skills is unequalled. *Team Canada* will have the opportunity to establish the superiority of Canadian players.

From the time the Russians splashed across the world hockey scene by defeating a Canadian team in the 1954 world amateur championships, Canadians have waited for the day when the Soviets played the top NHL stars. That day has arrived and *Team Canada* will display devastating offence as its main strength. The team's goaltending is first rate; the defence is sound. However, the club's shooters, a goal-scoring talent array of overwhelming potential, create the real excitement. Wrist shots, slap shots, backhanders, tip-ins, fakes — every method of scoring known is represented among 21 forwards who scored 735 goals last year and 3,522 in their careers. And they are backed by Ken Dryden, Tony Esposito and Ed Johnston, three of the premier goaltenders.

Phil Esposito is leading the parade. The centre of the Boston Bruins has scored 142 goals during the past two seasons. His specialty is positioning himself in the "slot" area in front of the goal where his size and strength make him difficult to move. Then, he converts linemates' passes with every shot in the book.

Montreal Canadiens' Yvan Cournoyer uses his tremendous speed to burst clear of defenders to unload his assortment of hard shots. His linemate, Frank Mahovlich, is the classic, elegant performer who can overpower the toughest defender, smoke a shot past the goalie or stickhandle in close for a shot with a wide, sweeping deke.

New York Rangers' Vic Hadfield quit trying to bomb long-range shots past the goalies last season, moved closer to the net and aided by his brilliant linemates, Rod Gilbert and Jean Ratelle, scored 50 goals.

Leading the young shooters, Richard Martin scored a record of 44 goals as a Buffalo Sabres rookie last season. Martin's slapshot is one of the NHL's best. It makes him a threat to score from any spot inside the blueline. He also has a deadly accurate, quickly released, wrist shot and abundant skating speed to make him a dangerous offensive player even though he's only 21 years of age.

To complement the strong scorers on the roster, *Team Canada* manager-coach Harry Sinden selected several lesser NHL stars for their specialized skills. For instance, Jean-Paul Parisé of Minnesota North Stars and Boston's Wayne Cashman scored 18 and 23 goals respectively last season. Their *Team Canada* chore is to patrol the flanks with Esposito at centre and supply him with the puck, obtained by their energetic digging in the corners.

In the modern NHL, defencemen play a key role in the attack, providing a hasty exit for the puck from their zone by passing it ahead to the breaking forwards, or rushing with it themselves. Defencemen now mix freely in the attack to produce frequent four-man onslaughts. Boston's brilliant Bobby Orr became the foremost attacking rearguard when he won the NHL scoring title, with 33 goals and 87 assists in 1969-70. Orr's participation in the Russian series is doubtful, because of a knee injury, but *Team Canada* has several skilled rushers on the blueline.

New York Rangers' Brad Park, the No. 2 defenceman in the NHL, counted 24 goals and 73 points last season. Park freewheels with the puck and has an excellent shot. Montreal's Guy Lapointe, New York's Rod Seiling and young Jocelyn Guevremont of Vancouver also are proficient offensively. Several strong defensive rearguards including Boston's Don Awrey, Bill White of Chicago and Detroit's Gary Bergman will balance the defence.

Frank Orr, The Toronto Star

The Team

Only nine of the 35 players on *Team Canada* plus manager-coach Harry Sinden have previous game experience against a Soviet national team. Sinden was a king-pin defenceman for Whitby Dunlops when they defeated the Russians on their way to the 1958 world amateur championships and he joined the Kitchener-Waterloo Dutchmen in the 1960 Olympic Games in Squaw Valley, Calif., beating the Russians but losing to the U.S. National team.

Centre Red Berenson starred for the 1959 world champion Belleville MacFarlands. Defenceman Brian Glennie was a member of the losing Canadian National team in the 1968 Olympics at Grenoble, France. Rod Seiling was in the 1964 Olympics at Insbruck, Austria. Goalie Ken Dryden played with the Canadian team against the Russians before it was disbanded in 1970. Mickey Redmond, Bobby Orr, Serge Savard and Gilbert Perreault faced touring Russian teams in games during their junior careers.

FORWARDS

Phil Esposito — The Russians will need more than a bearhug or Rags Ragulin's strength to dislodge 205-pound Espo from in front of the net; 30-year-old centre has 142 goals in last two seasons, an all-time NHL high; 76-goal season in 1970-71; first centre to make four straight first all-star teams.

Rod Gilbert — Reached peak in 1971-1972, scoring 43 goals; 97 points placed him fifth with total which would have won scoring title five years ago; right winger.

Bill Goldsworthy — One of two original Minnesota North Stars remaining from 1967; consistent scorer; over 30-goal mark three straight years; right winger.

Dennis Hull — Named to *Team Canada* because of devastating shot, said to be harder than brother Bobby's, though less frequent; is 27; scored 30 goals last year; 40 the year before; left winger.

Vic Hadfield — Rugged, "tough in the corners, erratic slap shot" was book on Ranger left winger till he abandoned slap shot and became 50-goal man last season; golf pro in off-season.

Yvan Cournoyer — Canadiens' Roadrunner has lightning speed; rugged despite size (5-7, 160); prolific scorer; 47 goals last year; always moving; right winger.

Wayne Cashman — Robust checker; diligent in corners; truculent to a fault; normally left winger for Esposito, moved to right side by Sinden for the series.

Jean Ratelle — Centres only one-team line on *Team Canada*; broken ankle ruined possible 50-goal season in 1971-72, but got 46 in 63 games.

Peter Mahovlich — Nine years younger than Frank, Peter

has put 35-goal seasons back-to-back for Canadiens; more extroverted than Big M; more truculent; less gifted on ice; left winger.

Bobby Clarke — Underrated Philadelphia centre showed ability in *Team Canada* camp; with Ellis and Henderson on wings, had No. 2 line; low-rated in draft because of diabetes; proved error of that decision with 35 goals for Flyers last season.

Jean-Paul Parisé — Hard working, unspectacular left winger who is strong defensively and excellent at procuring puck for more adept scorers; got 48 assists two seasons ago for North Stars.

Mickey Redmond — One of three Habs dealt to Detroit for Frank Mahovlich in 1971, emerged as star in his own right, last season with 42 goals; right winger.

Frank Mahovlich — One of game's most gifted men, enjoying rebirth of interest and stardom in Montreal after 11 frustrating years in Toronto and short tenure with Detroit; had 464 goals in 15 seasons; 60 of them in 114 games as Canadien; left winger; holds playoff record of 14 goals.

Red Berenson — Three-year head of NHL Players' Association has been with four clubs in nine years; now a Red Wing; dependable; once scored six goals in game for St. Louis; played for Belleville amateur world champs in '59; centre.

Dale Tallon — Vancouver Canucks' fine young utility man would prefer defence, but is playing right wing here; point production dropped in sophomore year last season but potential is great; so's size, 6-foot-1, 200 pounds.

Gilbert Perreault — Buffalo's first draft choice in 1970, set rookie record with 38 goals; as playmaker for Rick Martin last year, upped points total from 68 to 74; mesmerized Russians in exhibition as a junior in 1969; is 22.

Stan Mikita — Czech-born Hawk centre won NHL scoring title four times, second only to Gordie Howe's six; bad back has slowed him down in recent years; superb on faceoffs.

Rick Martin — Montreal junior went to Buffalo; broke Perreault's record with 44 goals, though losing rookie award to Dryden; just 21.

Paul Henderson — Leaf's left winger selected for good positional play; also matured as scorer last season, with 38; till then had great, unrealized potential.

Marcel Dionne — Another 22-year-old who might be best of lot; not as flashy; more complete player with strong defensive ability; despite slow start as rookie last fall, scored 28 goals, 77 points.

Ron Ellis — Scored 199 goals in eight seasons; 27 years old, stocky Maple Leaf right winger especially picked to handle his Russian opposite Kharlamov.

GOALIES

Ed Johnston — Boston goalie, 36, is oldest on *Team Canada*; in 10th year with Bruins; one of few holdovers from Bruins' lean years; was outstanding in *Stanley Cup* final this year.

Ken Dryden — Cornell all-American achieved "cart before horse" fame by being named top player in 1971 playoffs, the season before he was voted the top rookie; at 25, he's law student, goaltender; at 6-foot-4, one of biggest men in game.

Tony Esposito — Tony is 29, the more serious Esposito brother; set modern NHL record with 15 shutouts in rookie season; won Vezina Trophy in '72, second time in three-year career.

DEFENCEMEN

Gary Bergman — An eight-year survivor of turbulence in Detroit; reliable, cool, totally professional, best described veteran journeyman.

Pat Stapleton — His 279 assists in eight seasons underscore his playmaking ability for Chicago; on second all-star team 1971-72; held playoff assists mark, broken this year by Bobby Orr; former Hawk captain.

Bobby Orr — Boston wonder boy has won 12 NHL awards in six seasons, worth $69,875 in bonus money; League statistician may soon have to start a series of volumes on Bobby Orr's records; was first defenceman to win scoring title; three seasons over 100 points.

Brad Park — Being No. 2 isn't bad, when Orr is No. 1. Rangers' four-year veteran made first all-star team last season; scored 24 goals, 73 points; key man on power plays.

Rod Seiling — One of five Rangers with *Team Canada*; played in '64 Olympics; also capable winger; seven years in League at 27.

Bill White — Eight-year veteran of minors emerged as NHLer three seasons ago; has 135 points in League; reached peak with second team all-star nomination as Black Hawk in 1972.

Serge Savard — Plagued by injuries, he's missed almost three of six NHL seasons with Montreal Canadiens; named top playoff performer in 1969; potentially great if he stays healthy.

Guy Lapointe — He's 24, scored 49 points in second NHL season; has blistering slapshot; one of several good, young Canadien rear guards.

Don Awrey — Underrated in shadow of Orr; defensive defenceman who doesn't pile up points; Bruins' coach emphasizes consistency of this 29-year-old.

Jocelyn Guevremont — First-draft choice for Vancouver a year ago; was one of bright spots for last-place Canucks; earned 51 points as rookie.

Brian Glennie — Maple Leaf played against Soviets in 1968 Olympics; added to *Team Canada* after WHA defections reduced squad; knows international style of play; at 6-foot-1 and 197 pounds, can be physical defender.

Something of Value

Because he's both a Canadian and a hockey player, tonight at the Montreal Forum looms as a milestone evening in the life of Gordon (Red) Berenson.

The pressure of meeting the Soviets is not a new experience for Berenson, 31. In 1959, when he was attending the University of Michigan on a hockey scholarship, Berenson joined Belleville Macfarlands in their successful jaunt to the World Championships. Since then, the Russians have made enormous strides in hockey development, winning 11 world titles and three Olympic gold medals. Berenson has progressed to the front ranks of NHL centres with four different teams.

"Things have changed a great deal for us all since that day in 1959," Berenson said.

As a Canadian, Berenson sees this series as an important happening for the country.

"On Saturday night, Canada will be a very united country," he said. "All regional differences will disappear and the various peoples who make up Canada will be cheering as one voice.

"I doubt very much if one single Canadian will be cheering against *Team Canada*. Differences based on nationality or religion or any of those petty things which sometimes get in the way of this country's development will be forgotten.

"This series will get attention all over the world. We've always said hockey was our game, something of value that was unique for Canada. This is the first real chance to prove it and show the world something about our country."

As a hockey player, Berenson is extremely pleased to be a part of *Team Canada*.

"We're playing for Canada's hockey prestige on the world scene and the *Team Canada* players understand this," he said. "We've always talked about matching our very best players against the Russians and now we have the chance. We could say the timing of the series was bad for our conditioning program. We could claim that some top players like Bobby Orr and Bobby Hull weren't on the team. We could complain that *Team Canada* was a collection of players who didn't have time to jell into a cohesive unit. But, really, there can be no excuses. If we're good enough, then we'll be there. It's that simple."

Berenson feels that international competition will be a completely new experience for the *Team Canada* players, the majority of whom never have faced a team from another country. "We really have been isolated in the domestic competition of the NHL," he said. "There's a different atmosphere in international competition that's very difficult to explain. That first game in Montreal will be an enormous emotional experience for us and, I think, for the Russians, too. For us, that feeling will be more intense when we play in Moscow.

"You could sense that as our training camp progressed during the past three weeks. At first, the players were gratified to be chosen for the team but the games seemed a long way in the future. As that first one came closer, the players built up a genuine enthusiasm for the task as they realized the importance of it to them, both as Canadians and hockey players.

"I think that enthusiasm and the tremendous emotional drive the atmosphere those games will give us will compensate for lack of time we've had to prepare physically for this series."

When he was 19 years of age, Berenson found international competition to be a large learning experience. He apprenticed in the professional hockey-oriented Canadian system and the European approach was a drastic change.

"There was a different attitude of sportsmanship among the European teams than I was accustomed to. They were just as competitive as North Americans, but they were more complete athletes than we were. By this I mean that they took a hard-nosed approach to the game and played it to win. But they never seemed to lose sight of the fact that they were playing a game, almost in the British tradition of the meaning of the term 'good sport.' The Belleville team had several hard hitters and we literally knocked several opponents off the ice surface over the boards. But they never retaliated bitterly when this happened because they seemed to take the approach that it was just part of the game. I hope that atmosphere prevails in this series, but there's a strong possibility that it won't."

Frank Orr, Toronto Star

USSR NATIONALS

The Russians are Coming...

"In collective societies such as Russia, the player plays the board rather than his opponent." This observation was made as a comment on the Spassky-Fischer chess tournament by Dr. Kurt Adler, son of Alfred Adler and an exponent of his school of individual psychology. The comment is interesting in the context of Russian hockey. The Russian coach plays his team with strategy and tactics as a team of co-operating players who in turn play the puck rather than the man.

Hockey came to the Soviet Union after the Second World War, via Czechoslovakia. From the start Russian hockey was deliberate, studied, scientific. The Russians looked at our hockey playing for its moves and strategies. They looked for purpose; not for style, successful improvisation, or the sum total of individualities.

Where we have learned hockey by accident and improvisation, as a by-product of long winters with ice and nothing much to do, the Soviets have set out to rationalize and perfect offensive plays. Their offensive play, consisted of moving the puck ever-closer to, and ultimately into, their opponent's net. That was the first phase of Soviet hockey development, earning the Russians the reputation of funny guys who passed and passed the puck, and still passed it when they could shoot it on goal. Until a few years ago Russian hockey looked mechanical, automatic, exciting only in its near-perfect, offensive passing stratagems. It did not take long to become much more. (Russian soccer, handball and volleyball used to look mechanical too.)

Not long ago, Gump Worsley called the Soviet hockey players "a bunch of pea-shooters." Before the series began we knew that the Russian pea-shooting days were over, but to what degree few of us suspected until Game One in Montreal.

The Russian coaches Bobrov and Kulagin are members of the new generation of hockey players who learned the game under Anatoli Tarasov. This man did more than coach Russian national teams to many victories in recent years, he also wrote more serious hockey literature than anyone else. Tarasov saw a great deal of our kind of hockey in his day. He liked what he saw and studied it avidly. His conviction grew that hockey was not a game of individual improvisation but a collective effort in speed, passing and sophisticated team work. Within this collective effort, Tarasov developed what he considered ideal hockey players" . . . with the wisdom of chess players, the accuracy of snipers, and the rhythm of musicians . . . "

Tarasov found athletic ability and physical conditioning such self-evident qualities that he hardly mentioned them. He looked for and found, in short, NHL-type players at their peak who could be molded into a team and made to excel as a perfectly coordinated unit.

More than half the players of the *USSR Nationals* who came to Canada for the series were Tarasov players. Bobrov himself played with and under Tarasov. But Bobrov, who took over from Tarasov earlier this year, has a different outlook.

Milt Dunnell of *The Toronto Star* reported on the new look in Soviet hockey a few days before the start of the series.

H.W.H.

The Russians are Here...

As a military man, Col. Vsevolod Bobrov of the Red Army might be inclined to consider his present position as somewhat precarious. As coach of the Soviet national hockey team, he prefers to be philosophical.

After all, he reasons, no logical person should expect his team to sweep the eight-game series with *Team Canada*. He doesn't even discuss the possibility of the Soviets getting swept on their Canadian junket, followed by four home defeats in front of the top brass from the Kremlin.

Canadian partisans, some of whom obviously are being prompted by nationalism, rather than by knowledge of the competing clubs, have predicted eight straight wins for coach Harry Sinden's Selects. Johnny McLellan, coach of the Toronto Maple Leafs, and Bob Davidson, chief of the Leaf scouting system, both of whom looked in on the Russians during pre-season games in both Moscow and Leningrad, also agree on the probability of a Canadian sweep.

Mechanically, they insist, the Canadians have the fire power, know-how and goaling. The only question will be how well they adjust to international rules, the two-referee system and the amateur officials, all of which are strange to them.

As Bobrov maintains, no logical person would suggest his Soviets should wind up 8-0 against what *Pravda* describes as "the very flower of Canadian hockey." His peers might not be logical if the Russians should suffer what Muhammad Ali likes to call 'a whupping.' It would be so easy to recall that the Russians had been world amateur (with reservations) champions for nine consecutive years until Bobrov took over the head coaching chores from the demanding Anatoli Tarasov last spring.

Tarasov, also a Red Army colonel, had steered the Soviets to their third straight Olympic championship at Sapporo, Japan. He was replaced by Bobrov almost before the ceremonial vodka had been consumed.

Bobrov's first mission was to defend the World Cup, which had become a Soviet monopoly under Tarasov. The Czechs ruined Bobrov's debut by finishing first, with the Soviets settling for second. If Bobrov were to follow up that stinging defeat by getting clobbered in the *Team Canada* confrontation, he almost certainly would be in trouble, despite his international popularity.

Bobrov has captained the national soccer team, as well as the national hockey team — a rare achievement. He is the only hockey player to receive the Order of Lenin. In Soviet hockey, his stature would be equal to that of Rocket Richard or Gordie Howe. But can he win as a coach?

As the Russians and Sinden's Selects prepare to settle some of the arguments that have been raging for at least a decade, Bobrov's biggest problem well might be to determine who is calling the shots for his side.

Although Bobrov commenced a rebuilding program almost the moment he assumed command, it still is Tarasov's team. The big guns — Aleksandr Ragulin, Vladimir Lutchenko, Victor Kuzkin, Vladimir Vikulov, Aleksander Maltsev, and needless to say, Anatoli Firsov, all developed into Soviet celebrities under Tarasov. They will not change readily and easily to a new system — especially since they were so successful under the previous one. Firsov, whom most National Hockey League scouts have eyed with envy, could have been indicating the attitude of the veterans when he retired along with Tarasov.

In their coaching philosophies, Tarasov and Bobrov have widely differing views. To Tarasov, every individual had to be subjugated to the collectivism of the club as a whole. In his system, there was little room for stars. Ironically, Bobrov was largely responsible for this outlook. In the late Forties, before the Russians had emerged as a threat in the Bunny Ahearne version of international amateur hockey, Tarasov played on a forward line with Bobrov and Yevgenni Babich.

In the folklore of Soviet hockey, this line was the equivalent of the Cook brothers and Boucher or any of the other three-somes which were legendary in Canadian hockey before North American coaches resorted to platooning.

The Tarasov, Babich, Bobrov line operated on what Tarasov later called the 2-plus-1 system, which became standard in Soviet hockey. What he meant was that two men did most of the work — he and Babich, in this case — while the other member kept himself in position to make the shot on the net — and consequently get most of the credit. That was Bobrov.

Tarasov, an unglamorous workhorse type himself, recalls how he checked through press reports of games in which the line played. Invariably, it was Bobrov who was acclaimed as the hero in victory.

Tarasov's annoyance reached the boiling point in 1953, when the Russians were to have made their first appearance in the world tournament at Zurich. To the dismay of the players, the trip was suddenly was cancelled because Bobrov had taken ill and the Soviet bureaucrats had decided the national team would be humiliated without their big goal-getter. To Tarasov, this was an embarrassment to the other players — an admission that one man was bigger than the group. If he ever became a coach — as he intended to do — there would be fewer chiefs and more Indians.

Bobrov, a headliner throughout his career in two sports, soccer and hockey, naturally leans toward the star system. Quite aside from the fact that stars should inspire less talented teammates, Bobrov appreciates showmanship. He knows which type sells tickets. "My plan will be to make the maximum use of the individual styles of the players," he offered, during a luncheon discussion of the series with *Team Canada*, in Moscow, a few weeks ago. He grinned as he added: "I know you Canadians have said that we try to mold everybody into the group. I will be interested to hear what you think of our Maltsev-Kharlamov-Mikhailov line. This is a line which I think demonstrates my theory of exploiting individual styles. Kharlamov will stand out, even against your best Canadians. By North American standards, he is small but he has an excellent shot. I think he will be effective."

Valery Kharlamov is 24 — one of the young members of the Soviet team. He has averaged slightly less than one goal per game for the national team. Boris Mikhailov, also 24, has scored 58 goals in 87 games for the national team. Aleksander Maltsev, at 23, already has earned a reputation as one of the leading scorers in Soviet hockey. He is a graduate of Russia's junior European champions.

"I expect there will be some surprises for us when we meet your Canadian stars," Bobrov agreed. "Some things will not surprise us. For example, I know your goaling is superior. I know how your professionals like to place a successful scorer in front of the net.

"I have seen films of your professional games. They indicate to me that the player (Phil) Esposito will be difficult to move from the front of the net. He is big and strong. There probably are others."

By this time, Bobrov has exhaustive scouting reports on the Canadian team — prepared by Arkadi Cherneshev, a long-time partner of Tarasov in Soviet coaching, and Boris Kulagin, who will be Bobrov's assistant.

Cherneshev, a friendly, dedicated hockey man who is a keen student of the game, returned to Russia after watching two weeks of *Team Canada* workouts. Before he left, he was reminded of what Bobrov had said regarding the problem of keeping a shooter, such as big Espo, from intimidating his goalies.

Cherneshev grinned and said: "I see many problems out there." He nodded toward the ice. "There is so much talent. I hear it asked whether Bobby Hull will play. (He will not.) I hear it asked whether Bobby Orr will play. (He will.)

"When you have so many excellent players, I wonder whether it matters."

It does. Like Bobrov, Canadians are partial to the star system.

Milt Dunnell, The Toronto Star

The Team

FORWARDS

Vladimir Vikulov — Has 85 goals in 139 international games; at 26, three-time all-star in Russian first division; plays for Moscow Army; six world, two Olympic titles.

Aleksander Maltsev — He's 23, already established as a splendid prospect; experience and finesse of veteran; 87 goals in 94 internationals; three-time all-star with Moscow Dynamos; one of strong individualists with Soviet team.

Valery Kharlamov — Truculent winger of the Wayne Cashman school; also strong scorer with 77 goals in 89 international games; just 24; Central Army; three world, one Olympic title.

Boris Mikhailov — Bobrov tabs him one of stars; Central Army; 27; pro-style player, part of Russian new breed; moved up to national team after '68 Olympics.

Anatoli Firsov — Recognized as Russia's greatest player ever; now 31; retired after this year's Olympics; returned for chance to play NHLers, but reportedly knee injury will keep him out of games in Canada; 111 goals in 150 games; strong, fast, tough; pro-type shot; played for Tarasov's Central Army team; now coaches with him; earlier attempt to lure him to NHL here failed.

Vladimir Petrov — Young veteran at 25; 61 goals internationally since 1969 when he joined team; played 88 games.

Viacheslav Starshinov — Record of 135 goals in 165 international games; from Moscow Spartak; retired, but recalled for Canadian tour; he's 32; never any doubt of his ability to play North American pro hockey; tough and great; his stick may have saved Russians' championship in 1967 when it injured Carl Brewer's eye.

Yuri Blinov — Newcomer of 23; 15 goals in first year; Moscow Army for three straight USSR titles.

Yevgeni Zimin — Defensive stalwart; from Moscow Spartak; he's 25.

Yuri Lebedev — A 21-year-old freshman from Wings of the Soviet.

Yevgeni Mishakov — At 31, Moscow Army veteran would be pro standout; one of new coach Bobrov's individualists, capable of improvising as well as playing disciplined, mechanical game which has been Russian trademark; four world and two Olympic titles.

Aleksander Yakushev — He's 25; from Spartak; 28 goals in 80 international games; with Soviet teams in 1967, '69, '70 and '72.

Viacheslav Solodukhin — From Leningrad, 12 goals in 13 games as rookie national in 1971; 22; one of top young stars.

Viacheslav Anisin — Also 22; from Soviet World Student champs of this year; plays for Wings of the Soviet; limited international play to date.

Aleksander Bodunov — Rookie; 21; from Wings of Soviet; first international event.

Vladimir Shadrin — Reserve; from Spartak; on World University champs of 1968; he's 24; has 23 goals in 43 games.

GOALIES

Vladislav Tretiak — Relative newcomer at 20; grad of crash course for goalies as Soviets weak at position; junior international; joined big team last year; Moscow Army.

Aleksander Sidelnikov — From Wings of Soviet, he's 22; first time with nationals.

Viktor Zinger — Veteran of many international tournaments, he was recalled to national team when Vladimir Shepovalov, 24-year-old rookie from Leningrad, was injured.

DEFENCEMEN

Aleksander Ragulin — Big Rags is veteran of 210 games with world champs; return to domestic all-stars in Moscow after three-year absence, indicates he still has touch; plays for Moscow Army; strong shot from point; 26 goals in world play.

Vladimir Lutchenko — One of several rising youngsters; 23, but all-star two years in first division; with Central Army; three world titles and one Olympic gold medal.

Viktor Kuzkin — Veteran at 32; Central Army; member of nine national, eight world and three Olympic championship teams.

Yevgeni Paladiev — From Moscow Spartak, he's 24, rejoining national team after two-year absence; former USSR all-star.

Aleksander Gusev — Twenty-five-year-old rookie national; three years with Tarasov's Army team.

Gennadiy Tsigankov — Another of many Army team members on squad; 41 international matches; with '72 Olympic champs and world tourney runners-up.

Valery Vasiliev — Moscow Dynamo skater who graduated from Russia's European junior champs; three years with nationals.

Vitaliy Davydov — Thirty-three-year-old veteran; has played on six world champs and three Olympic winners; world all-star in 1967; compact build, much like Pat Stapleton.

Yuri Liapkin — Star rearguard for Moscow Spartak; joined Nats in '71 global win.

THE TEAMS

CANADA	RUSSIA

GOAL

CANADA	RUSSIA
35—Tony Esposito	20—Vladislav Tretiak
1—Ed Johnson	27—Aleksander Sidelnikov
29—Ken Dryden	1—Viktor Zinger

DEFENCE

CANADA	RUSSIA
2—Gary Bergman	5—Aleksander (Rags) Ragulin
5—Brad Park	7—Gennadiy Tsigankov
25—Guy Lapointe	3—Vladimir Lutchenko
3—Pat Stapleton	4—Viktor Kuzkin
17—Bill White	26—Eugeny Paladyev
23—Serge Savard	25—Yuri Liapkin
16—Rod Seiling	2—Aleksander Gusev
26—Don Awrey	6—Valery Vasiliev
4—Bobby Orr	14—Yuri Shatalov
38—Brian Glennie	

FORWARDS

CANADA	RUSSIA
20—Peter Mahovlich	10—Aleksander Maltsev
19—Paul Henderson	18—Vladimir Vikulov
6—Ron Ellis	17—Valery Kharlamov
28—Bob Clarke	16—Vladimir Petrov
10—Dennis Hull	13—Boris Mikhailov
12—Yvan Cournoyer	9—Yuri Blinov
7—Phil Esposito	Pashkov
22—J. P. Parisé	Astafyev
18—Jean Ratelle	Volchkov
8—Rod Gilbert	19—Vladimir Shadrin
9—Bill Goldsworthy	11—Eugeny Zimin
14—Wayne Cashman	15—Aleksander Yakushev
21—Stan Mikita	12—Eugeny Mishakov
24—Mickey Redmond	21—Vyacheslav Solodukhin
15—Red Berenson	22—Vyacheslav Anisin
27—Frank Mahovlich	24—Aleksander Bodunov
32—Dale Tallon	23—Yuri Lebedev
34—Marcel Dionne	

GAME ONE

The Impossible Nightmare

"How much do you want for Kharlamov?" asked Toronto Maple Leaf owner Harold Ballard. He stood at the edge of the rink in his Gardens stadium. He had difficulty pronouncing the Russian name.

Not in the least disconcerted, Vsevolod Bobrov, coach of the USSR Nationals, dispensed with the interpreter, stared for a few moments, grinned, and asked in competent English: "How much will you pay?" The grin turned into another blank stare.

Cheque book in hand, his normally gruff voice raised an octave or so, Ballard replied: "One million and a future draft choice . . ." One of the bystanders whistled.

Coach Bobrov, on skates, disengaged himself from a near-embrace, moved back on the ice to his players and gestured them into activity.

Ballard turned to his audience and said: "Well, they all have a price . . ."

It was the day of Game Two, a Monday, with the result of Game One in Montreal, the previous Saturday, still very much alive and hurting. The morning papers carried banner headlines about the first Team Canada-USSR Nationals *encounter . . . Oh, Canada . . .! Disgrace . . . Defeat . . .*

The score: seven to three for the Russians.

It was the day after one Toronto newsman had swallowed every shred of his column in which he had predicted an eight-game sweep by Team Canada. *Most Canadians still had some swallowing to do.*

Reports said that comments in Moscow had been factual, calm and of minor importance. "The hockey myth has been shattered . . . Canadian players are not invincible . . ." There were no reports of political or ideological rhetoric, official statements, blatant glee, the interruption of public affairs or any variation in the normal flow of life in the Soviet Union on our day of woe.

From the Russian point of view, their team had gone to Canada to face a challenge issued by Canadians for high purposes of state; accepted by the Russians as a matter of course. Whatever important reasons the Russians had in coming, if they had any, we shall probably never know.

One Team Canada player was to say later: "Those Russians play a game . . . they have no heart . . . no emotions . . . no stakes . . . they just play, and play and play . . ."

They had come to Canada . . . carrying their own bags, unsmiling, regimented, with equipment that drew condescending smiles, drinking only orange juice . . . to play, they said, a series of friendly games and to learn much from the Canadians. Our propaganda machines fed us the lines, the facts, the impressions . . . with a little bit of smugness and a faint touch of condescension. The Russians went to bed early, stayed together, cast only furtive glances at the fabled beauty of Montreal's womanhood, practised, and went to see The Godfather. *They looked very young and stern and a little vulnerable.*

That was before the first encounter on ice.

"They have no heart, no emotion, no stakes . . ."

"They all have a price . . ." someone else said. Or may we believe that Mr. Ballard only spoke as a member-owner of the NHL whose cooperation made it all possible?

H.W.H.

What are the ingredients of what normally ends in laughter? How about starting a game at home, with 18,818 fans ready to raise the roof . . . the Prime Minister looking on approvingly . . . and 30 seconds into the game — a scramble, and goal! How about a second goal six minutes and two seconds later when Paul Henderson's shot along the ice catches the Soviet goalie dreaming of a White Gorky Street? By this time, *Team Canada* has one-and-a-half shots — and two goals. The first was scored by Phil Esposito. Bring out the adding machine.

Could that be the darling of the Volga, Eugeny Vladimirochich Zimin catching Dryden on his derrière in the 12th minute? And what's this? The Soviets, who have taken their third penalty in a row, have separated Gilbert from the puck and now Boris Petrovich Mikhailov is testing Dryden and Vladimir Vladimirovich Petrov is scoring. The Soviets are giving us the chill!

There's a kid on this Soviet team named Valery Borisovich Kharlamov. He's slightly under 5'6", and weighs 150 pounds. He's a left-winger. In other words, he's roughly three quarters the size of Frank Mahovlich. Anyway, if Boston defenceman Awrey is looking for a reason why he's not in the lineup for game two, he can blame it on Valery. In the third minute of the second period, Kharlamov swept around Awrey in a one-on-one no-contest and beat Dryden for the go-ahead goal.

Midway through the period, it's the pocket-sized Kharlamov again. This time, he takes one step into the circle to Dryden's right, and the big goalie fans on the shot.

Don't get the idea from all this that *Team Canada* didn't have scoring chances. Among Esposito's 13 shots at the goal and seven on, four could have beaten most goalies. But not Vladislav Tretiak. And while the Soviets left *Team Canada* all the way down to HERE in the area of conditioning, it should be mentioned that Team NHL was at its best during a three-minute span in the third period.

For example, Clarke's goal at the 8:22 mark made life worth living again, and also when Henderson and Hadfield

followed with near-misses . . . But then the Mahovlich-Cournoyer-Esposito line was left hanging in the Soviet zone while Mikhailov (top shooter for the Soviets with six shots) scored the backbreaker. This one went through Dryden's legs. Then, less than a minute later, it's Zimin again. Alexander Yakushev, a rather large 6'2" and 180 lbs., completed the rout by taking Dryden for a cup of coffee. Down goes Dryden and up goes Yakushev's shot. A backhander.

The book of etiquette will mention that *Team Canada* did not adhere to the bold print in the waning seconds of the game. Guy Lapointe became involved with one of the Soviets, who didn't really like the idea of being shoved by Lapointe. Esposito then elbowed the reluctant Russian, and then skated several feet to elbow another, who was watching the shoving. Elsewhere, Clarke slashed Alexander Maltsev with a two-hander across the ankles. The crowd's reaction? Loud and long applause for the Soviets, a thunderous chorus of boos for Esposito.

"Cheap shots?" Sinden was asking yesterday in reply to a question. "The Soviet team can teach us a few things about cheap shots. If a hockey fan's eye were trained like a hockey player's, he would see many things that we wouldn't get away with in the NHL. We're not saying they took cheap shots, but we're not gonna let anybody say we did, either!"

Red Fisher, The Montreal Star

Humble Pie

There is something about the battered-looking skates of the Russian hockey players, something about their refusal to mix it up with *Team Canada* players and their insistent reliance on skilled teamwork that must ring in the memories of most Canadians.

Who can't remember his own battered skates? His hockey glove taped over where there was a hole in the thumb? His coach who, unlike so many of the current variety, would bench a player for provoking a fight? The brilliant stickhandler who would sooner shoot than pass — and who lost games that way?

It's early in the series, but as we digest the humble pie served up by the Russians on Saturday night, and as *Globe and Mail* columnist Dick Beddoes eats his column, as he promised he would if *Team Canada* didn't win 8-0, we can't help wondering about the team spirit of the Russians.

If Valary Kharlamov were getting, say, $2 million and if Alexander Yakushev, Eugeny Zimin and Vladimir Petrov

33

were each negotiating for even more, who would be passing to whom?

Editorial, Globe & Mail, Toronto

Deficiencies

Hockey is more than a game to Canadians, because it is — or so we fondly supposed until Saturday night — the one form of human endeavor in which we are the world's best. It is an important ingredient of our national pride, and an expression of our national character.

Instead of blaming our side for inept play, let us reflect a little on what *Team Canada's* humiliating loss to the Russians tells us about ourselves as Canadians.

First, about our capacity for self-delusion. Seldom since Goliath contemptuously looked at David can an opponent have been so grossly underrated as we underrated the *Russian Nationals*. All Canadians concerned — players, coaches, Hockey Canada and National Hockey League executives, sportswriters, sportscasters and fans — shared in this error.

A pre-game commentator said this was "the greatest team ever to represent Canada." If he had said it was the greatest collection of individual stars ever to play for Canada, the statement would be indisputable. But the Russians were about to demonstrate what the word "team" means; their vastly superior teamwork, and equally superior physical conditioning, were the foundations of their victory.

Of course, these advantages owed something to Canadian overconfidence. If the Hockey Canada organizers had even faintly anticipated the strength of the Soviet team, they presumably would have negotiated with the NHL for more time to get the *Team Canada* stars working as a unit and in top condition.

But there is probably a more fundamental reason for *Team Canada's* deficiencies here. The rampant commercialization of hockey in North America has more and more glorified individual stars, at some cost to team spirit and team play. In their world hockey debut, our pampered professional darlings played as if they had scarcely been introduced to one another, and were outclassed by Russians who earn tiny material rewards by NHL standards.

Is it too much to expect that $50,000- to $100,000-a-year hockey players should be in shape in September, like the Russians? In a country where physical fitness is the exception to the rule among the general population, and where hockey stars constantly receive uncritical, gee-whiz

hero-worship, it probably is. We built them into the legendary figures who were so methodically humbled by the Russians Saturday night, and should not blame them too severely for turning out to be merely human.

In one sense, a deeper humiliation than Saturday's loss befell Canadian hockey before the series ever started. Most players on *Team Canada* — or more precisely, the NHL All-Stars — are representing this country by the grace and favor of 12 American clubowners. We deluded ourselves by supposing that we could sell our national game — like our national economy — to the highest bidders and still excel in our own right.

At least *Team Canada's* overconfidence has been brusquely dispelled, and we can expect it to play more carefully, with due respect for the Russians' capabilities, from now on. Whether it can sufficiently overcome its deficiencies in team play and conditioning in the remaining seven games will determine the quality of this series. If *Team Canada* loses, let us not accuse it of letting Canada down. In its shortcomings, as in the "Owned in U.S.A." brand on most of the players, it probably represents us all too faithfully.

Except, we may hope, in the matter of decent manners and sportsmanship. *Team Canada* added disgrace to humiliation Saturday by taking cheap shots at the Russian players (who responded with admirable self-control) in the final minutes of the game, and by failing to stay on the ice for post-game handshakes. It would be idle to deny that there is a tradition in Canadian hockey of trying to assuage the pain of defeat by fouling and fighting opponents. But must our pros act like bush-league soreheads when they skate into the world arena and lose? If we must lose, let it be with some grace.

Editorial, The Toronto Star

Top Marks to the Soviets

Well, the question of whether Soviet hockey is the equal of the NHL has been eloquently answered. Now the question for the remainder of the eight-game series is: Can NHL hockey match the Soviets.

Every hockey fan in the world—including Soviets—must have been rocked by that 7-3 Soviet triumph in the first game. That first one was the important one, the big one. And forget the explanations, the rationalizing, the second-guessing. It's results that count in this cruel world, not "if onlys".

Top marks to the Soviets.

Everything was stacked against them for that first game. Consider: the change in time zones; brand new playing conditions; a vociferously partisan crowd; exposure to NHL super-star reality after years of propaganda. And then the psychological crusher—the first Canadian goal in 30 seconds. A lesser team would have crumbled right there.

No, the Soviet victory was earned and deserved.

Maybe *Team Canada* will bounce back. That's not the point. The point is that Soviet hockey established itself.

Whatever the results of the remaining games in Canada, the biggest test for our boys will be in the four games in the USSR—in the other guy's rink, so to speak.

The broader ramifications are clear. International hockey is now of NHL calibre. The *Stanley Cup* is no longer emblematic of world supremacy. Perhaps now it's time to have an "open," international trophy for the world's best.

Anyway we have a tip for Coach Sinden on how he can beat the Russians: Harry, you gotta find a way to get Bobby Fischer into your line-up!

Editorial, The Toronto Sun

Too Funny for Words...

Has anybody ever invented a new way to say "I told you so?" I tole you and I tole you, Massa, them buzzsaws don't fool. Maybe it is the virulence of the Russian toilet paper, like the professors say. Or the whole way of life: the rundown skates that the fortune's darlings of our own sports system thought were just too funny for words when they saw them at Friday's practice; the kids (including some on this Soviet team) who never have owned a car.

However, if you are the sort who is interested only in the narrow nationalistic concept of *Team Canada* rather than in the game itself, don't shoot yourself yet. The NHL All-Stars might suddenly recall, from the mists of the distant past, what hockey as a game was intended to be about. They knew it once. They've got two arms and two legs and a head each, just like the Russians. Also, some are quick learners and shouldn't need more than one immersion

course in the game's old verities, such as they got on Saturday night.

But would the people please stand up who have been sneering for years that the Russians were afraid to play our pros? And that's why the attempt two years ago to allow the Canadian team to use nine professionals fell through? And who said then that the Soviets were shamming when they contended that they wanted to play our best, but only if it would not affect their Olympic standing?

Of course, many Canadians who fell for that anti-Soviet guff were only repeating nationalistic and largely ignorant claptrap that was being served up by the majority (although not an unanimous majority) of Canadian sports pages and broadcasts. Puberty comes hard to some people. As a result, many have scarcely noticed even yet the orderly procession of Soviet moves.

They were genuinely worried about Olympic eligibility, exactly as they said. So they got the 1972 Winter Olympics out of the way. Then they simply said, "Okay, we're

ready." They didn't impose prudent conditions. They shot the wad.

They *wanted* to play against Phil Esposito, Bobby Orr, Bobby Hull, Frank Mahovlich, Stan Mikita; all of whom they read about from childhood in their sports magazines at home. They wanted to play the best — and believe this, too, they were prepared to lose eight straight games if in doing so they improved their hockey skills by playing, as they say (rather quaintly, in the circumstances), "Against the stars."

I thought the Soviet team might lose the first game simply because of being over-awed. That would have been natural enough. I was sure they would win a few games later in the series. As it turned out, there was an uncanny resemblance early in the game to one 14 years ago in Maple Leaf Gardens, the first exhibition in this country between these two hockey powers.

That time, the Russians scored twice in the first 70 seconds. Then Whitby Dunlops picked themselves off the ice and came back to win it 7-2. It was almost the same, in reverse, Saturday night. The first two quick goals and you think, "Geez, it could be a 10-0 or more." But in this game the Soviets controlled the puck even when they were down 2-0. From then on they played what Punch Imlach calls "that funny game where they don't let you have the puck."

Punch is one of quite a few good hockey men, incidentally, who did not take the Russians lightly. He and I spent a long afternoon a couple of years ago with Andrei Starovoitov in Montreal. At the end Punch was convinced that if Starovoitov ran Soviet hockey, which he does, the Soviet desire to play the pros was for real.

The thing that shamed me, and I guess many of us, was not the loss. That was nothing — one team playing hockey at it best and deserving to win.

But when grown Canadians wearing their nation's name on their backs get chippy, cheaply chippy, I feel badly for us.

The night when we show we can't dish it out, we show that we can't take it either.

That was bad, and if *Team Canada* worked and lived together for three weeks without finding out that they, or at least their game star Bobby Clarke, were supposed to stay on the ice at the end of the game, like sportsmen, what the hell did they spend the time doing? Because obviously they didn't spend it preparing soberly, in a self-disciplined way, to play the kind of hockey that was needed to win on Saturday night.

Scott Young, The Globe & Mail, Toronto

Shattered Myth

When our national institution crumbles with one Bolshevik bodycheck, what then can preserve the adjacent out-buildings of our culture? Nothing. Our national inferiority complex, defended only by our hockey, may now become terminal neurosis.

No, I'm not calling it a conclusion with seven games to go. After all, we won a few face-offs and killed several penalties. But, after the dark date of Sept. 2, 1972, is chiselled in marble by weeping historians, we'll never be the same. We are unlikely again to be so . . .

"Arrogant and conceited," Douglas Fisher put it tersely.

Our haughty outlook changed forever during a meaningful span early in the second period that lasted no longer than five, maybe six seconds. It was 3-2 Russia and none of us was yet convinced that Team NHL wouldn't soon bring down all its wrath and power upon the impudent invaders.

Then it happened. Alexander Yakushev, a 190-pound Bobrov Bobcat, jolted Ron Ellis with a classic check that sent him to the bench with fluttering wings. Seconds later, Valery Kharlamov knocked Guy Lapointe to the ice with a thump . . . and then — and then Gary Bergman iced the puck!

Whatever Team Canada had presumed about the Russians (and it's a safe bet they presumed nothing more than a playground picnic against comparative novices), their notions had altered with the manifest admission: "Ice the puck, brother, these cats have got us on the run."

Canada will come back. With each furiously-paced game, more oxygen will reach the lungs and more red blood will fuel their legs, but Eagleson's All-Stars will never forget this hardy lesson. Russia not only acquired their respect, they demanded it in no uncertain terms.

"We were stunned . . . absolutely stunned," Harry Sinden said.

Sinden and his squad are left to sing an operetta of the obvious. And the rest of us, too. For every Canadian who cackled in anticipation of a chauvinistic coup sur glace, the Russians proferred a streak of speed, a brilliant pass, a robust bodycheck, a gallant save.

To say we took Russia lightly is to hear General Custer ask: "What Indians?" We spotted the challengers playing dates the most favorable to them and the least favorable to us, clucking confidently that we'd clean 'em anyway. Our invincible image now lays bare, a myth.

Ted Blackman, The Gazette, Montreal

Russian Delight

Andrei Starovoitov was wearing his best Gorky street suit and dourest expression in the moments after *The Embarrassment*.

You may remember Andrei. He is, to Soviet hockey, a Clarence Campbell with muscle. When Andrei says Stanley, his entourage says Cup. When he says Right, the people around him say Guard. A pretty nice and knowledgeable guy, by the way.

Andrei has a long memory. It stretches all the way from Moscow to the garage in the Forum, which is where *The Embarrassment* was being explained on Saturday night. What better place than a garage to repair roughly 20,000,000 flat tires?

Andrei produced the barest hint of a smile as we shook hands. It started at the corners of his mouth, which is where most smiles start. It reached about a centimetre toward the left and right earlobes.

"You told me in Moscow," he said, "that the series would go in eight straight games."

"I remember that too well."

"You may be right," he said.

Andrei earned the right to deliver that blow to the gut. After all, didn't all the puff language up to game time have a decidedly western twang to it? A stunning 7-3 wipeout by the Soviet team — and he earned it . . . just as a Tass man named Viacheslav Chernyshoff had earned the right to say after the first period:

"It reminds me of a Buffalo-Boston game."

And after the second period, with the Soviets ahead 4-2: "I have changed my mind," said Viacheslav. "It is not a Buffalo-Boston game. It is Switzerland against Boston!"

Back off, Andrei! Scram, Viacheslav! Wasn't it bad enough for a guy who had called it in eight straight to see a 2-0 lead disappear? Is it really necessary to clunk a guy over his throbbing head with a samovar?

If you're looking for excuses, forget it! There aren't any. Anybody who even hints that *Team Canada* played badly is wearing the flag on his sleeve. Goals aren't scored to the tune of the National Anthem. The Soviets, on Saturday, were just too damned good. They took their 'weaknesses' and jammed them down our throats like all-day suckers. They made us like it.

I don't know about you, but I awoke yesterday morning and started wondering whether all of it had been a bad dream. I suspect that Harry Sinden awoke to the same feeling. Probably worse. His face was white and his hands fidgeted with a microphone late yesterday afternoon when he greeted the curious. I'll say this for Harry: there were no shallow explanations; no weak excuses.

"How do I feel? How do the players feel? There's a feeling of surprise, I think and acknowledgement. I think that's good. You should have respect for your opponent, otherwise you don't play up to your potential. There's no doubt what we're up against now. On Saturday," he said, "we ran around trying to be everywhere the puck was. When you run around doing more than what you're supposed to do . . . that comes from being too high. That's where we ran into all sorts of trouble."

Sinden sighed heavily. "It's a real competition now," he said. "It wouldn't have been worth a damn if it was easy. On the other hand," he grinned tightly, "maybe they're not thinking it's so much fun because it was easy."

"I wonder," he said, "how much they learned from us last night! ! !"

Red Fisher, The Montreal Star

GAME TWO

Everybody Came Back

Move over and make room for *Team Canada*! That loud noise you heard around 10:30 last night came from 35 hockey players — and perhaps 20,000,000 Canadians — exhaling all at once!

"We played a more sensible game," said Harry Sinden, after his "new look" NHL All-Stars put it together for a 4-1 victory over the *Soviet Nationals*. "We didn't run around like we did in the first game. We had control in positional play. I think our changes helped."

Helped? Does Rockefeller earn a living wage? Can Mark Spitz swim?

The name is Tony Esposito, and when the Canada-Soviet series opened on Saturday in Montreal, he was a spectator. Now it's two nights later, and the gun is levelled at his right ear-lobe because if the Soviets handle *Team Canada* the way they did in their 7-3 series opener . . .

Anyway, there's no score in the first period and Brad Park is in the penalty box. A kid named Alexander Maltsev sweeps down the wing to Esposito's left, flips a quick pass to Valary Kharlamov, who ruined *Team Canada* with a pair of goals on Saturday. Kharlamov catches the puck and in one motion snaps it at the open side to Esposito's right. Tony turns it aside with his skate.

One goal doesn't make a game, but in last night's game, one goal is all that was scored for two periods. And in the first period, at least, Tony was IT with several brilliant saves.

The changes helped?

Wayne Cashman is the name, and if there was one major part of the *Team Canada* game which was laced with cavities on Saturday, it was in the area of hard-nosed, aggressive forechecking. There's a rumor going around that last night, Cashman body-checked a Soviet player in the warmup — he was that aggressive. Nothing that caught the referee's eye particularly, but the blood in Cashman's eye was like a red light to the Soviets most of the night.

"He had them looking," agreed Stan Mikita, who was another "change" last night. "He had a lot of them looking, because with Cashman playing the way he was, a lot of our other guys simply picked it up from there. Look, there was this one time when Bobby Clarke went after a puck in the corner. A little guy, see? There's this big Soviet defenceman who has eight strides on Bobby, and he's eight strides away from the puck when he stops and looks. When somebody as big as that stops to look for Bobby, it means they're thinking. They're looking."

"That was the most impressive thing about the game," agreed Ken Dryden, who wasn't dressed last night. "Tony made those two big saves in the first period, and then we started to take control with our aggressiveness. I had the feeling . . . even when we led by only 1-0, that we had taken control. People were coming back tonight. Our defence played exceptionally well . . ."

Changes? Serge Savard was one of the "new" defencemen, along with Pat Stapleton and Bill White. He started slowly, but by midway through the first period, he was an eye-catcher. The big strides . . . the body now and then. Even the spin-around he has used so frequently and effectively against NHL opposition.

"All through training camp," Savard was to mention, "I didn't think we really put enough emphasis on defence. All the time, it was goals . . . . goals . . . how many goals are we going to beat them by! Score! Score! But tonight, we brought some defence back into the game. Everybody was coming back and it made it a lot easier for the defencemen. If we skate . . . did you see that Cournoyer go around Ragulin? . . . we can beat them. We can't beat them eight straight now, but we can come close. If we play like we did tonight . . ."

Skating and work. That's what brought *Team Canada* its first goal. And give most of the applause to Cashman for this one.

It's in the eighth minute of the second period, and a delayed penalty is called on the Soviets. The puck springs loose and Cashman races for it, undressing a Soviet defender on the way. That included the defenceman's stick. Cashman has the puck in the corner, works his way beyond the stickless defenceman and gets the puck to Esposito. Phil finds an open corner.

Remember Savard talking about Cournoyer's burst around Alexander Ragulin? It happened in the second minute of the third period, at which time Gannady Tsygankov was in the penalty box. He was a forlorn figure there, but not a lonely one, because he had Kharlamov as company, the latter serving a 10-minute misconduct for stealing a page out of the professional book and pushing the referee. Cournoyer gets the pass half a stride behind Ragulin and sweeps in on Vladislav Tretiak, who has been something of a heroic figure for the Soviets thus far in the series. This time, Tretiak has his legs open just enough to allow Cournoyer's shot to get through.

If you're thinking that the Soviets decided to flip onto their backsides, snap a Russian obscenity and quit at this point, you haven't been reading the latest memos from the Kremlin. The Soviets simply don't do these things. But just like other human beings, they start looking when they hear the thunder of skates. They even kick up a little snow now and then. But they skate . . . and shortly after Bobby Clarke was caught slashing at 5.13, Eugeny Zimin was on his way, unmolested, toward Tony Esposito from centre ice, shot wide, but was able to break into a gold-toothy grin from sideburn to sideburn when his great and good friend Yuri Liapkin got the puck to Alexander Yakushev about six feet in front of Tony.

Here it is with something like 14 minutes left in the third period, and now Pat Stapleton is heading for the penalty box. There's only one goal separating the teams now, and ALL our side really is hoping for is that Phil Esposito and Peter Mahovlich can kill off the penalty. You can't depend on this Mahovlich, however. Ask him to do a simple thing like killing off a penalty, and he'll go one step farther. As a matter of fact, he went many steps farther. Esposito started the play by getting the puck to Mahovlich on this side of the Soviet Blueline. That's Poladyev waiting for him . . . and then looking at Peter's retreating back. Peter fakes to his left, moves to his right, and could that be an empty net he's staring at? You betcha!

The Soviet game may not have gone to pot at this point, but it started to look a little thin at the seams. Vyacheslav Starshinov made it officially by giving the puck to Frank Mahovlich, and Peter's brother caught the far corner. He also patted Vyacheslav on the back for his generosity.

Red Fisher, The Montreal Star

Losing Bets

As soon as I walked into Maple Leaf Gardens last night I was haunted by this "on edge" feeling. Like I was about to take a toboggan trip down a giant size razor blade — with a toboggan.

Yikes!

Quickly, I sought out confrere Dick Beddoes, of the Toronto Grope and Flail. I had to know something right now!

"Dick," I said. "When you ground up your *Globe and Mail* column and ate it in a bowl of cold borscht on the steps in front of the Russian Embassy, after Saturday's game . . . did you do it for real, or did you pretend?"

He gave me a sickly, green smile.

"They just shredded it and mixed it right in," he said, gagging on the words. "I don't know how I got it down, but I haven't been able to eat a damned thing since."

Then he started laughing for real. "Hey, you're not worried about losing your bet, are you?"

"No," I lied, "just curious."

There was a newspaper sitting in one of the pews along press row. I walked over, checked around to see that no one was looking, ripped off a corner and popped it in my mouth. I began to chew it slowly. I looked furtively around again, and decided to try and swallow it. I gagged . . . my eyes watered . . . and I spat it out.

"Oh gawd," I groaned, "I can't believe he ate the whole thing."

Oh well . . . "Go . . . (gulp!) Canada (barf!) Go! ! !"

And sure enough, they went.

And if they get up and go just two more times like they did last night, well . . . bring on the Russian dressing and let's think of a name for that little printer's devil of a dish.

How about . . . Salad Mahovlich?

Red Fisher has been covering the NHL for 19 years, or 18 years and a few months longer than I have. He blew his prediction of eight straight for Canada, in the very first game. He even had the good sense not to back it up with any grandstand play.

So tell me, then, why is he even more nervous than I as we walk into Maple Leaf Gardens? Why are we both giggling like two schoolkids during the two national anthems.

I'll tell you why. It goes back to something Red said to me before tucking me in with my milk and cookies (a new union side benefit) the night before.

"Do you realize," he said, "that we could well be witnessing tomorrow night the single most important game in the 50-year-history of the NHL? One more 7-3 pasting by the Russians and it's all over . . . And I'll spend the rest of my adult life wondering why I wasted half of it covering a minor league. Haw . . . it can't happen. But dammit, it did happen once. And that's what scares me."

John Robertson, The Montreal Star

Remember How It Used to Be?

One cold November day nearly four years ago, one small incident cast a long shadow ahead for me to the hockey series that now is taking place between Canada and the Soviet Union. The scene was a courtyard in one of those endless rows of Moscow apartments; built like a hollow square so that children have a place that is off the streets, a place where their grannies can glance from a window and see that little Slava is keeping out of trouble, and where the parents coming home from work can stand a while and watch the kids at play.

The kids this day were playing hockey on a patch of incredibly rough and chewed-up ice. Some were playing with real sticks, others with the broken ends of sticks, some on skates and some on overshoes, some with toques and some with fur hats, their schoolbags and coats tossed carelessly nearby.

It made me think of a blizzard-swept service station where I stopped in Manitoba one winter, and found the kid who was manning the pumps had a goalnet set up and was hammering shot after shot at some board targets. It made me think of a farm boy I knew who had flooded an area in the barnyard and, if he couldn't get anyone to play with, had his big black Labrador dog trained to fight him for the puck and try to take it away from him. It reminded me of endless winter scenes in Canadian towns and hamlets where exactly the same thing happens every winter, and did to Dick Duff and Frank Mahovlich and hundreds of thousands of other Canadians who, by their very numbers, were bound to produce the ones whose names would become famous.

Watching the courtyard game in Moscow, I said to the Russian with me, "It is like Canada." And then got thinking that there were one heck of a lot of those courtyards for Russian kids to start playing the game.

The point is, there is nothing unnatural in a country the size of the Soviet Union producing in the last 25 years the kind of team that can challenge and sometimes beat our best. They have something like 8,000,000 boys playing the game each winter in registered leagues; and millions more in what they call courtyard hockey, and we would call shinny.

They don't organize theirs at as early an age as we do. There isn't any of this business of 8-year-olds in full equipment in leagues labelled tykes or atoms or whatever. But every city, town and village has its sports clubs and in winter they flood everything that is floodable and then let nature take its course. When a boy is 13, if he is good enough, he goes on a registered team for the first time. That bantam group, for ages 13-14, is his introduction to system. If he continues to progress, he'll make a team in what they call juniors: ages 15-16. And if he still keeps on, he'll be on what they call a Youth team, ages 17-18.

Some are good enough as Youth team players, to get an occasional game with a senior club, but there is no attempt to rush them along. Each sports club is like a pyramid, with the most teams in the lowest age group, fewer in the next one, still fewer in the next, and the senior team sits on top with all these developing young players from whom to draw.

It is at this point, graduation to senior hockey, that most changes from one club to another take place. For instance, if a graduating Youth player for the Central Army club

team in Moscow isn't good enough to be a regular for the elite army team, and doesn't want to ride the bench, he might move to another club. This can be done simply by writing a letter to the Soviet Hockey Federation; after which the federation checks with the coach the player wishes to leave, and the one he wishes to join. In the final decision, the aim is to do what is best for the player. A couple of years ago one of the best defence pairs for Moscow Dynamo were both, in effect, rejects from Central Army—and in league games were doing their best to haunt their former club.

But that is all simply mechanics. The real heart of Soviet hockey development is in system.

Soviet theoreticians long ago broke down the game into its main components—skating, shooting, passing, checking—and began to teach. In skating and passing they were helped by the old Russian game called bandy, played with a ball and bandy sticks (like field hockey sticks) on flooded soccer fields, with 11 men to a side. Former bandy players were transformed into the first team players in what the Soviets call puck-hockey. They could all skate like the wind. Other puck-hockey skills were harder to come by, but about 1947 they began the long haul up to where they are today, when their players have never played bandy, or known any skating game except puck-hockey.

There aren't anything like as many artificial ice rinks per capita in the Soviet Union as in Canada, however, so many parts of the training program have to be carried out without ice.

You'll find a hockey forward line of, say, 15-year-olds, in a gymnasium, recreated as a basketball forward line; their hockey coaches running the show and keeping the same boys together, on the grounds that passing techniques, and getting to know one another's moves, can be learned as well in one game as another. Five-man soccer is used in the same way: the same forward combinations as in hockey, same defence pairings.

Once on the ice, they have training methods never seen here (although Hockey Canada has made many valuable moves in the direction of scientific coaching). They practise skating at full speed, diving to the ice, and jumping to their feet again in an instant. A couple of times in Montreal this phase of training showed. They practise skating while being held from behind. Their defencemen go through long three-on-two workouts in which only the forwards have sticks; the defencemen must use their bodies and skates entirely.

All these coaching and training techniques are taught at national coaching courses. There's little or none of our volunteer-dad type of coaching at any Soviet hockey level. The coaches write exams, reports on games, player assessments; and may be granted holidays from regular work to travel to Kiev or Moscow or other major centres for brushups and refresher courses.

The results are now among us. The Soviet players in Canada now are drawn from many teams, as ours are. Back home on Moscow Army, Spartak, Dynamo, Wings of the Soviet, Gorki Torpedo, Leningrad Army, they play against each other—and often in league games, players we've never heard of are the big stars. So if the NHL All-Stars are the tip of one iceberg, the Soviet Selects are the tip of another.

All those courtyard kids in overshoes were bound to catch up to us, eventually.

Scott Young, *The Globe & Mail*, *Toronto*

You Can't Have Everything

It will be a blessing in disguise if our hockey team loses the whole series to the Russians.

We have become altogether too puffed-up, bumptious and arrogant about who we are and what we can do. Canada's most attractive virtue used to be her modesty, a beautiful quality in a country or a person. We were better than we knew, or let on, and that's a nice way to be.

But modesty became in the lingo of chauvinism something called a national inferiority complex. Now, to feel inferior without cause, that's neurotic, that's a complex. But to feel inferior when you are demonstrably less distinguished or meritorious than others, that's not neurotic, but plain self-awareness and common sense. If our art, our science, our industry, our gross national product fall considerably short of the major nations', as they do, shouldn't we accept the fact rather than pretend otherwise?

In athletics, to take the present case, isn't it a fact we always fare badly at the Olympics, that we have to import most of our football players—and baseball players, now that we have one team in the big league? Our record of world championships is scarcely something to brag about. In Munich, an American, Mark Spitz, has taken seven gold medals, while the whole Canadian team isn't expected to win any.

"It is a national disaster," declared Harold Ballard when *Team Canada* took a shellacking in the opening game. The *Star's* Jim Proudfoot, reporting from Munich a day later, restored our perspective by raising a nice cheer for Abby Hoffman's performance in the 800-metres. Abby finished last, but she ran a great race, in the best time she's ever made for that distance. Good for her, and for us.

As for hockey, yes, we have been unbeatable in the past, but surely that's been because no other nation bothered to play the game. If England or one of the European countries wanted a team, they imported Canadian players.

In the U.S., the game was marginally popular as a spectator sport, but not something the average kid got into. Again, Canada was expected to supply bodies for the pro teams.

Masters of the game for so long by default, we must now adjust ourselves to the reality of Russian pre-eminence, if not in this series, certainly within a few years. The Soviet Union has, what, 220 million people, a climate even colder than ours and a tradition of soccer excellence that is now being carried into hockey.

This is a team sport and in team sports discipline, constant drill, conditioning, professionalism (ironically, we're the pros) mean more than individual brilliance and dash. In chess, the very opposite's the case; that's the reason Bobby Fischer was able to overwhelm the superbly coached Spassky.

With our small population, we can't expect to throw up a chess genius, either. We're not in the big time of sports or any other endeavor you can name. What of it? We have a good country. We are, in fact, a very lucky people.

You can't have everything.

Dennis Braithwaite, The Toronto Star

GAME THREE

Soviets on the Ropes
Canadians Swinging

What's the dialogue during the coffee break today, folks? Are you warming up the cyanide? Breathing a sigh of relief?

Did you think, as so many people thought here, that after leading 3-1 and 4-2, *Team Canada* GAVE it away? There were mistakes by *Team Canada* — after all, how does anybody explain two short-handed goals? But *Team Canada* didn't give it away. The Soviets TOOK it away!

"Aren't we all glad to be alive to watch that kind of hockey?" Harry Sinden was asking after the NHL All-Stars and Soviet Nationals emerged with a 4-4 non-verdict.

Translation: *Team Canada* probably was glad with a tie, even though the shooting margin belonged to Canada, 38-25, and even though *Team Canada* did, indeed, hold two-goal margins at various points of the hockey game.

Team Canada had the Soviets on the ropes last night, but ended up swinging and almost strangling.

They got an early goal from Jean-Paul Parisé, even though the Soviets took a page out of the *Team Canada* book and forechecked the Canadians with vigor in the first couple of minutes. But then a short-handed goal by Vladimir Petrov at 3:16 stunned *Team Canada* momentarily and even appeared to arouse them.

If *Team Canada* had a period in the game during which everything fell into place, it was during the last half of the first period. They got only one goal out of it — by Jean Ratelle — but the pressure was on. The hitting was fierce. The forechecking worked. Only the superb goaltending of Vladislav Tretiak kept the Soviets alive and healthy for their second-period assault, which produced a 3-1 margin in goals and established the tie.

"I don't know what it is . . .", mused coach Sinden, "about those shorthanded goals. Maybe we're too anxious on our power-play." Maybe. But the Soviets have demonstrated they can turn it around even with their rib-cages against the Winnipeg Wall.

It's in the 13th minute of play. By that time, *Team Canada* has a 3-1 lead, and could have had a couple more. Tretiak, for example, saved brilliantly on Ron Ellis at the eight-minute mark. . . . Then Alexander Maltsev is stopped magnificently by Tony Esposito, and that seems to arouse *Team Canada* even more.

There's a kid named Yuri Lebedev on this Soviet team. Last night was his first time in a game of such importance, along with line mates Vyacheslav Anisin and Alexander Bodunov. A few months ago, they were part of a student team which played in Lake Placid, but last night they were on the ice against *Team Canada* and at the 11-minute mark, Lebedev has a delayed penalty.

Serge Savard and Guy Lapointe have good cracks at Tretiak. He stops them both. The pressure is on, though, with *Team Canada* striving for another goal, and then it happens. Gannady Tasygankov is in the corner. He passes the puck across the ice, where it's banked off the boards and deflected on the stick of Valary Kharlamov waiting alone at centre ice. Goodbye! Brad Park can't catch him and Esposito can't stop him. It's now 3-2, and even though Paul Henderson provided *Team Canada* with another two-goal margin at 13.47, the Soviets took less than five minutes to get the two goals they needed.

Remember the students? They did their homework well. First, Lebedev at 14:59, and then Bodunov, at 18:28.

After that: life and death, even to the point where Maltsev once had the puck behind Esposito, only to have Park get there before the puck crossed the goal-line. And another time, Kharlamov and Mikhailov BOTH were behind Esposito, and in their anxiety, managed to shoot the puck out of danger.

Where, oh, where was the positional play of Monday night? *Team Canada's*, that is. Was it a case of *Team Canada* losing its cool in the opening moments, or was it a case of the Soviets figuring that if it worked for Canada Monday — why not for the Soviets on Wednesday?

It appeared more of the latter than the former, even though it was Parisé who scored the first goal. All the way . . . it was Parisé, going behind the net for the puck, muscling a defender off it and getting the puck back to Bill White. A high shot — and what's this? Could that be Tretiak giving up a rebound? The puck bounces to the ice and Parisé is where he should be. So is the puck.

Frank Mahovlich will not include the Soviet goal among his treasured memories. Valary Vasiliev is in the penalty box for elbowing, of all things, and Mahovlich has the puck at his blueline. Cournoyer is on a break down the right side, but Mahovlich misses him and passes the puck back to one of the *Team Canada* defenders. He gets it back. Now, he passes the puck to Vladimir Petrov, who doesn't happen to be a member of *Team Canada*. (One of the fundamentals of hockey — professional or amateur — is to pass the puck to a man wearing the same sweater as you do.) A 40-footer snapped through Esposito's legs.

What turned it around in the last half of the period? Hitting, probably. Some of the hitting may have incurred the displeasure of European referees, but . . . anyway, it was turned off. And so was the Soviet pinpoint passing. Turned off to the point where they allowed people like Cournoyer and Ratelle to sweep in with two-on-one breaks.

"It's a good sign," murmured Red Berenson. "We had to wait until the second period before we took over. Now we've got them on the run after only half a period, right?"

Wrong!

Berenson was wrong, because while *Team Canada* was exerting some pressure in the first half of the second period, it was downhill all the way after that. It's true that Henderson had a goal picked off by Tretiak in the opening moments of the final period. But after that, the only real attention attracted by the NHL All-Stars was when Wayne Cashman rapped Yuri Shatalov over the helmet with his stick, and managed to attract a minor and a misconduct for his trouble. Cashman and Shatalov had been conducting a fairly active rumble almost from the start of the game, but Shatalov won it by default. At 10:44, Cashman was out of it, and the Soviets were making life miserable for *Team Canada*.

What did last night's game all come down to? Was it a matter of *Team Canada* running out of petrol? Probably. It also was a matter of several players not even approaching the all-out effort of Monday night's victory. Mahovlich (Frank) had a bad night. So did Park. Tony Esposito didn't have much of a chance on any of the goals, except for the 40-foot short-handed goal that went through his legs, but he was fighting the puck from the start.

Red Fisher, The Montreal Star

Comrade & Friend

With only 13 seconds remaining in a game that had the hockey fans of two continents reaching for the tranquilizers, Alexander Nikolavich Maltsev whipped a shot from a soggy spot 20 feet to the left of the *Team Canada* net.

Tony Esposito, the shutout king of big league hockey in North America, reacted slowly. His view was screened by the mass of sinew and bone that was churning and wrestling, bobbing and weaving, almost to the edge of his goal crease.

At the final flicker of an eyelash, Tony spotted the puck and made a save. His brother, Big Phil, most prolific shooter in a league that once was considered to tower higher than Mount Everest over any other circuit in the world, was checking Maltsev.

Phil had frozen in his stance, toe to toe with the Soviet star, as the shot was delivered. Maltsev also had stopped dead in his skate tracks.

Both players sensed this could be the knockout punch.

When Tony smothered the puck, the mask of horror on Phil's face changed to a wide grin. He looked Maltsev in the eye and gave him a friendly pat on the shoulder.

The Russian shook his head and smiled. It was an exchange of thoughts without words.

Maltsev was saying to Phil: "Comrade, you could have won but you almost lost."

Phil was saying to Maltsev: "Friend, we should have won but we're damned happy to settle for a draw. Twice, you were two goals down. Don't you know when you're licked?"

Milt Dunnell, The Toronto Star

Too Freely Enterprising

Presumably Harry Sinden picked Wayne John Cashman for Team U.S. NHL the other night because he knows Cashman has the muscular resolution required for mock war against the *Soviet Union Selects*. Cash is no peacenik, to be sure.

Coach Sinden would have been kinder, however, to pay Cash off with 50 lashes and a paddle on his bare behind.

Ever since the Canadians tied the great skate-shoot series for the championship of two-legged animals at 1-1, Cash has been flayed as though he is an ogre who would drink Russian blood at body temperature, or near there.

Charles Templeton, speaking into a patch of CKEY ether with the well-known sports expert Pierre Berton, got off a simple, straightforward salute. "Cashman played against the Russians like he meant to kill," Templeton said approximately. "I mean kill." Chuck made Cash sound like a meat-eating-type fella, and no mistake. Cashman listened to the glowing critique of his work as he rode to Maple Leaf Gardens for a morning practice. "I don't usually listen to such garbage," he said, "but we had the car radio on. Those two guys must go to ballet." As to that, this department doesn't know. I do know that if I had been editorializing on violence in sports yesterday, I'd more likely have deplored Arab terrorists literally killing Israelis at the Olympics in a bloody display of corrosive hatred. I probably would have taken a columnar swing at the Maoist bums who assaulted policemen with clubs outside the Gardens.

If you are going to knock violence in sport, it says here, there are larger contemporary targets than Cashman. All he did was reef a few Russians, who, being over here for friendly competition, reefed him in return. Just the same, the readers in Omsk and Outer Mongolia must be asking, "Who is this monster, this despoiler of homes and corrupter of youth, that he is horsewhipped thus?" The answer is, "He is a tall chunk of gristle from Kingston who plays left or right wing the best he knows how for the Boston Bruins." The best he knows how was learned on the playgrounds and rinks of Canada, where most of us learned games. Most of us learned very young that

the best and most natural retort to make to an adversary is a punch in the snoot.

I can remember, pretty vividly, getting cuffed around fairly often in a prairie schoolyard by a tough kid named Ray Carmichael and hollering at him through bleeding lips, "Aw, who d'you think you are? Eddie Shore?"

Now Cashman had finished 90 minutes of brisk practice and was surrounded by a cluster of reporters. His lean physique was draped in a red, white and blue shirt with belled sleeves and cream slacks with flared Western cuffs. He didn't seem particularly dangerous standing there, talking quietly, unless you are blinded by fancy duds.

"Hit hard in hockey?" Cashman responded to a question. "Hell, you can get hit harder when somebody suddenly opens a door and bangs you on the nose."

He said what anyone would say who has focused even casual concentration on the Russians. "They stop you by getting in front of you. They tug at you and hook and hold to stop you. Get in front of them like I tried to and they've got to tow you with them. That can get tiring."

Cashman mentioned what should have been obvious to anyone who wasn't half asleep or half in the bag. "The Russians are all strong and they can all take a check and give you a pretty good going over with their sticks."

That wasn't a Canadian who chippily slammed U.S. referee Steve Dowling into the boards, Chuck and Pierre. That was clean living All-Soviet Valery Kharlamov, a swift, agile left wing. While he was incarcerated for 10 minutes in the penalty box, the Canadians scored three of their four goals in a 4-1 conquest.

The Russians long ago discovered that hockey is not precisely a game for convent girls. They, like Cashman, seem to accept the premise that hockey is a combat sport and reason that when a man has the puck he leaves himself open to being vigorously hit. Or even when he doesn't have the puck.

There seems no way the Canadian players can win, however. Lose, as they did Saturday, and they get whacked. Win, as they did Monday, and they get whacked. We are curiously cannibalistic, forever ready to eat our own young.

One woman telephoned Sinden's office yesterday to complain about the Canadians chewing gum during the playing of the national anthems. After the game, Sinden received a congratulatory wire from Vancouver: "Nice going. I'm an agent for Barnum and Bailey and spotted some great talent on your team. I need some clowns."

There is nothing clownish about Cash, as Tim Burke wrote yesterday in the *Montreal Star*. "There's nothing like a little Cash," Mr. Burke wrote, "to get the free enterprise system going."

Dick Beddoes, The Globe & Mail, Toronto

GAME FOUR

Is There a Proud Canadian in the House?

Perhaps the Godfather, who is Alan Eagleson, summed it up best before Game Four:

"The only thing I don't like about this series," the executive-director of NHL Players' Association was saying, "are the games!" Eagleson liked them even less after Game Four. A 5-3 victory for the Soviets provided them with a 2-1-1 record for the games in Canada. It also provided them with one more victory than they had hoped for.

The victory was rarely in doubt from the time the Soviets moved into a 2-0 lead on power play goals by Boris Mikhailov — both while Bill Goldsworthy was in the penalty box. Deservedly so each time.

This was the first time in the series that *Team Canada* had to play catch-up hockey from the start. And while they managed to get a goal in the second period from Gilbert Perreault after a great end-to-end rush (the puck finally going into the net from an impossible angle off defenceman Valery Vasiliev), there was no time, really, when *Team Canada* threatened to take over in any way.

The goaltending was not the type of goaltending normally produced by a Ken Dryden. There were moments when he, alone, held off the Soviets, but there were other moments when he appeared shaky.

Dryden's analysis: "The Soviets shoot quicker than NHL players. They start moving around a defenceman and while an NHL player would do the job and then shoot, the Soviets seem to release their shots while they're moving around the defencemen. And this business about them not shooting hard . . . perhaps collectively they don't shoot as hard as this (*Team Canada*) team, but they can shoot as hard as the average NHL team."

Dryden touched on this area of the Soviet game. But there were others in which they left the NHL trailing. Many others . . .

At no time, after *Team Canada's* first goal, did the Canadians get closer than the one-goal margin. Yuri Blinov scored while Pat Stapleton was caught up the ice, and before the period was over, the Soviets had a 4-1 margin on Vladimir Vikulov's goal. Earlier, a *Team Canada* goal had been disallowed when the referee ruled that Rod Gilbert kicked the puck into the net.

Goals by Bill Goldsworthy, the Soviets' Vladimir Shadrin and Dennis Hull came in the final period, with Hull's goal scored with only seconds remaining in the game.

The Soviet style in Game Four was little different from the first three games of the series. Skating, of course, was of paramount importance. Defensively, they made errors now and then, but they still appeared stronger than their opposite numbers.

Passing? Once again, they had it. As usual, they didn't shoot quite as often as they should have, waiting, instead, for more of a "sure" thing. That would come under the heading of a man moving into the slot when the puck-carrier was beside the net, or in a position where he didn't have what the Soviets considered a good shot at Dryden.

It was clockwork — precision work. There were shots off-target, of course, but there were many more which barely missed or which forced Dryden into excellent saves. In capsule form, a fairly one-sided game — a game in which the Soviets simply skated away from *Team Canada*.

The reaction? Monstrous in the eyes of *Team Canada* players in that the Vancouver crowd hooted the Canadians frequently. They brayed at Dryden now and then.

"It was frustration on their part," shrugged Dryden.

They directed sour cries at Bill Goldsworthy, after his two penalties led to Soviet goals.

"I'm ashamed to be a Canadian," snapped Goldsworthy.

The braying reached its loudest when Frank Mahovlich held onto goaltender Vladislav Tretiak when the goalie came out of his nets on one occasion.

"I was puzzled at that reaction," Mahovlich mentioned later. "I held on to him because the net was open. I saw the puck at the blueline and I figured that if I held a little, maybe a goal is scored. On the other hand, why should I be surprised? The whole series has surprised me! And didn't the crowd give the Russians a louder cheer before the game began than we got? How do they (the Soviets) manage to do this? They must have a politician behind the bench!"

Clearly, the adverse crowd reaction nettled most *Team Canada* members. "Unfair," was the way Phil Esposito put it after the game, "and something we didn't deserve. We gave up a lot for this series . . . money . . . our vacations. Mind you, I'd do it again tomorrow if I were asked, but we didn't deserve it!"

The jury will have to remain out on that assessement. The braying was strange and, no doubt, a source of irritation to the athletes. But it's not the first time a losing team has been the object of disaffection. The only difference here, perhaps, is that it's a case of Canada-vs-Russia. If applause and acceptance were measured strictly on the merits of which team played better, the Soviets deserved what they got.

The fact is, the Soviets monopolized the play, pressing and, when they needed it, getting superb goaltending from Tretiak.

It's 3-1 for the Soviets in the second period. Yvan Cournoyer is sent into the clear on a great pass from Rod Seiling. He's 20 feet in front of Tretiak when he releases one of his great shots, and the goalie stops it.

It's the same shift. Cournoyer gets into the clear again,

and this time — properly — Cournoyer decides that he's going to stickhandle into Tretiak's territory. After all, a searing shot hadn't beaten him seconds earlier . . .

Tretiak beats him again.

"All that guff we heard about the Soviets . . . they beat us good," said Espo. "They beat us fair. The scouts . . . they should give up scouting. And that goaltending. Did I hear somebody say that their goaltending was supposed to be weak? Hell, he reminded me of Dryden the year the Canadiens beat us in the playoffs."

Vladislav Alexandrovich Tretiak, a married man of recent vintage. Twenty years old, six feet, one inch, and 180 pounds, he's as tall and as unemotional as a stalk of Soviet wheat. Going into last night's game, he had allowed 11 goals in three games, which is not the type of goals-against average that wins *Vezina Trophies*, but what it does win — and has won in this series — is a respect and admiration for something that wasn't supposed to exist. Even by the admission of Soviet coaches themselves, goaltending has been the weakest part of their game, but Tretiak has turned it around. All the way . . . even with 11 goals in three games.

Let's go back for a moment to Game Three. It's late in the first period and *Team Canada* is leading 2-1. By this time, *Team Canada* has unsettled the Soviet team to the point where Tretiak is the only one left to defend against Jean Ratelle, who scored 46 goals in the National Hockey League last season, and against Frank Mahovlich, who has been among the league's great goal-scorers.

Mahovlich is in the slot, about 15 feet in front of Tretiak. There are a couple of Soviet bodies screening him from the Soviet goaltender, but the shot — a quick backhander — is stopped. Tretiak had to move on the play, but he got there. Then, seconds later, there's a scramble in the Soviet goal-crease. Ratelle has the puck . . . then he doesn't have it any longer, because Tretiak has reached out and taken it away from him.

It's the second period, and by this time the Soviets are behind 3-1. They're behind because Tony Esposito has stopped fighting the puck long enough to take away a goal from Maltsev. Now Ron Ellis is in the slot, 25 feet in front of Tretiak. Once again, there are bodies in front of the Soviet goaltender. The shot is hard, quick and accurate. Tretiak traps it between his pad.

"I watched Tretiak in Leningrad," Toronto Maple Leaf coach John McLellan was saying before the start of the series, "and he wasn't good. How is a goalie supposed to look good when he's beaten 8-1?"

What is it about goaltenders that makes the good ones better than average and the better-than-average goaltenders outstanding? The outstanding goaltenders win games under pressure by making giant-sized saves under pressure. Tretiak, who was not considered proficient enough to do

these things, has been doing them.

"I am not surprised at the way Tretiak has been playing," insists Vesevolod Bobrov, the Soviet coach-in-chief. "For the big games . . ."

"That's what has impressed me most about him," says Ed Johnston, who is the No. 3 goaltender on *Team Canada*. "The pressure doesn't seem to bother him at all. I don't think he's super-human. Eventually, it will get him. He's young now. He'll learn what pressure is, but you look at him out there and if he gets a bad goal scored on him . . . I thought we had him that first game . . . it doesn't bother him. That's only part of it, though. How many rebounds has he given up? He stands up there and he traps the puck in his pads and people are waiting for the puck to pop loose — and nothing happens.

"How would he do in the NHL? Let's say that he's doing pretty well against their best right now. I thought that when some of our big guys started shooting at him, he'd be looking for the door to his dressing room; guys like Cournoyer and Mahovlich and Ratelle would run right over him.

How would he do? He's 20. He's only 20 and he is doing this to us! !"

It was the goaltending, all right, but it was much, much more. If the Soviets had to rely strictly on the goaltending, they would not now be leading the series. It's easy to say that the goaltending turned it around for the Soviets, but the last time anybody looked, Tretiak hadn't scored any goals for his team. He did his job, and others in front of him did theirs.

Many, many Soviets did their jobs, and not enough Canadians were able to do theirs. Not because they didn't try. Perreault, for example, was a fairly strong performer, particularly for a first game. And Esposito once again was the work-horse, the brilliant individualist. It was Espo who did most of the work on the last two Canadian goals.

But it wasn't enough . . . not nearly enough.

Red Fisher, The Montreal Star

Big M's Cold War Vision

Frank Mahovlich checked into room 1012 of the Bayshore Inn and immediately began tapping the walls and peeking behind the drapes as the bellhop gaped incredulously. "Shhhsh," he whispered to Serge Savard, his bunkmate. "Don't say a word — this joint has gotta be bugged by their agents."

Serge nodded gravely. Two days ago he was laughing at the Big M and his growing paranoia. Now Serge isn't so sure Big Frank isn't right.

"I wouldn't be surprised at anything the Russians would do," Mahovlich says, speaking seriously as his eyes scan the twilight zone. "No sir, I wouldn't be surprised if they were training a football team at a secret army base. They'll beat the Dallas Cowboys next year."

Phil Esposito guffawed. "They might win the U.S. Open, too," Espo said. "Can you see Jack Nicklaus booming one of his 350-yard tee shots and then a Russian guy . . ."

Six or seven of Esposito's teammates laughed. Mahovlich didn't. Later, when the Big M had left the circle (darting down the hallway to elude the secret agents), Savard said: "Have you ever seen Big Frank act this way? He's going crazy over this series."

He isn't alone. So profound has been the shock of the Russians' arrival as peers that the slick Canadian professionals have had their senses scrambled. One week ago they watched the Russians practise and mocked them. Yesterday they leaned over the boards and studied each move intently.

"It was a con job, a beautiful con job," Bobby Orr says. "I saw them at the Forum in Montreal last week and I felt sorry for them. Their lousy skates, stumbling over the blueline, fanning on shots. We were going to beat them so bad I actually felt sorry for them."

Russia, it now becomes evident, played on Canada's anxiety to reclaim its lost prestige. When the Canadians came calling with an offer to play our pros, the Russians feigned ruluctance . . . agreeing only after every condition was outlined in their favor.

At *Team Canada's* training camp, two Russian scouts filled notebooks with diagrams and wore awestruck masks. During their first practices over here, they stumbled through routines in pitiful equipment and terrible techniques.

"What a con job, eh?" Bobby Orr says.

And a psyche job, too. Hardly an hour passes without the Russians knocking on Harry Sinden's door with another complaint. Practice is too early; practice is too late; the opening ceremonies are too long; they're not long enough.

"Watch it, Harry," Frank Mahovlich keeps telling his coach. "Watch it. Be prepared for anything. This is a cold war, you know. A cold war. I've had hay fever for a week now. In Toronto, Winnipeg and Vancouver. How can the pollen count be so high everywhere I go?"

"Maybe," Eddie Johnston suggests in jest, "they're following you around with a powder in a spray can, just to upset you."

Sinden chuckles.

"Don't laugh," Frank says. "They'll do anything."

They've got to Frank, or he's got to himself. In the second game, the Big M was far removed from character He dumped a Russian after the first-period buzzer, banged a few guys on the helmet with his stick, patted the veteran Vyacheslav Starshinov on the back after he'd scored for Canada.

If Mahovlich reads a sinister plot into everything the Russians have done in Canada, he is unquestionably convinced that cloak-and-dagger treachery lies ahead. Mention the Moscow end of the series and the Big M's imagination begins to parallel Ian Fleming's.

"What we should do in Russia is camp outside the city, all of us in tents or something," Frank was telling Savard the other day.

"Hell, what for?" Savard wondered.

"Don't you think they might just start a construction project outside our hotel room at four o'clock in the morning? Just to ruin our sleep?"

"Most of the guys aren't in by that time," Savard said, trying a joke.

"Don't laugh. You don't realize what this series means to them for propaganda purposes. They'll do anything. We should buy some tents."

Frank strolled off for a coffee, leaving Savard in a perplexed slump on the lobby couch. Mahovlich is a great put-on artist. Serge wonders if he's being taken. Then he remembers that strange, faraway look that is in Frank's eyes every day.

Savard turns to Eddie Johnston, asking: "Do you suppose he may be right and we should . . ."

Ted Blackman, The Gazette, Montreal

Games Adults Play

Jim Coleman loves his trade. He is a venerable sportswriter, loving sports and words with equal abandon. In the wake of the Winnipeg game, he had this to say.

"In this crisis the chauvinists will not help by second-guessing Harry Sinden and neither my media colleagues nor I will help matters by reporting that players are complaining about being left out of the lineup; or by reporting that players, suffering from acute frustration, are taking the odd dollop of schnapps."

After the Vancouver defeat, the second defeat for Team Canada, he reported as follows. "Forget about that little 5-3 defeat in Vancouver . . . We're just lulling those Russians into a sense of false security . . . The Canadian spectators are proving to be of invaluable assistance in the perpetration of this masterfully conceived subterfuge. Some of the Canadian spectators are booing our hockey players—thus deluding the Russians into believing that Canada has lost confidence in our team. The Russians are gobbling up the bait like lagniappe. By the time they get back to Moscow, they'll be so over-confident that they will fall into our trap . . . Even some of our hockey players are contributing to this sly scheme. Phil Esposito did a grand job . . . pretending publicly that the boos of the Canadian spectators were irritating him . . . It seems to me that this would be a very appropriate occasion for the Canadian hockey fans to grow up, overnight, and begin to act in the manner of mature adults . . . Really there is not much to choose between these two hockey teams . . . this particular Russian team has been playing over its head in this series . . . the Volga boatman had better get busy and start bailing—because his ship is going to be sunk without a trace . . ."

And again after the second game (Team Canada won the first 4-1 and tied the second 4-4) against the Swedes in Stockholm:

"In a performance which left North America's professional hockey players exposed nakedly to worldwide ridicule, Canada was forced to score a short-handed goal in the final 47 seconds of play to scratch out a humiliating 4-4 tie with a team of Swedes who had been training for only 10 days. Worst of all, the Canadian hockey players failed to comport themselves as mature professionals. Displaying about as much poise as a drunk at a WCTU picnic, they permitted the Swedes to goad them into penalties which reeked of abysmal stupidity. As a matter of fact, when Phil Esposito scored the tying goal at 19:13, Vic Hadfield was serving the final seconds of a five-minute penalty which he had received for performing unlicensed surgery on defenceman Lars-Erik Sjoberg in front of the Swedish net. It is true that Lars-Erik had been clutching furtively at Hadfield's elbows, but this undetected misdemeanor scarcely entitled Victor to give Sjoberg a palpably obvious cross-check which left him bleeding copiously from the mouth. Hadfield's penalty was by no means the most stupid of Canada's sins, but coming as it did with Sweden leading 4-3 at 14:31, it left our side in one hell of a bad spot. The Swedes had capitalized on penalties to Phil Esposito and Jean Ratelle to score their third and fourth goals earlier in the period . . .

"Egad—I'm sounding angry, and I don't intend to resort to indignant recriminations. Nevertheless, next week's junket to Moscow is beginning to assume all the outlines of a gruesome comedy. The Canadian team which was tied by Sweden last night would be stoned, ten-to-zip, by the Russians. The unpardonable sin, as I see it, is that the Canadians have forgotten that their compatriots on the other side of the Atlantic Ocean expect them to act as mature adult professionals. We can forgive them being beaten by the Russians—and tied by the Swedes—but we don't expect them to completely lose their composure when they are taunted by lesser opponents."

Jim Coleman never had any doubt that Team Canada would win the series. He took a strong stand against the Stockholm interlude which, he wrote, will do nothing for the Canadians and may well get them in trouble.

Still in Stockholm, the morning after . . .

"You should have been here in 1969, when the young amateurs of Canada's National Team made their last appearance in a world hockey tournament. The bewildered young Canucks were subjected to a newspaper campaign of vilification which exceeded the bounds of sanity. They were accused of being animals and incipient sadists.

"In the context of 1969, Monday's patronizing comments merely were irritating. The papers carried headlines such as: "*Team Canada* Disappointment?" "Canada Glamor Wears Thin;" "Three Crowns (Sweden) The Best Team;" "Esposito Threatens Kjell Svensson?" "They (Canadians) Were Playing Like Gangsters." The last-mentioned tasty little item was the heading on a column purportedly written by Ulf Sterner, the aging star of the Swedish team. Sterner's journalistic effusion of Monday certainly was a flagrant case of the pot calling the kettle black. By comparison, Sterner makes Marlon Brando's Mafiosa Godfather resemble Father Christmas. Sterner, who has improved his surreptitious stiletto technique immeasurably since he defected from the New York Rangers some years ago, is a master of sneaky infighting.

"Wayne Cashman made the great mistake of skating halfway across the ice to crash Sterner into the boards on Sunday night. Sterner met him with a honed stick-blade which sliced Cashman's tongue as neatly as if the operation had been performed with a scalpel. If Cashman hadn't staggered back in surprise, Sterner was quite ready to perform a tonsilectomy for an encore.

"And it is a bit amusing to read of Sterner deploring all

these gangster tactics when you're aware that Sterner and Benny Anderson leave today to attend the training camp of the Chicago Cougars of the WHA. Two other members of the peace-loving Swedish national team, goalie Leif Holmqvist and defenceman Arne Carlsson, will follow them to the Chicago camp later this week.

A day or two later, this prelude to Game Five of the Canada-USSR series in Moscow—(a traditional man-in-the-street-with-policeman encounter):

"They think that it is Grey Cup night."

"Grey Cup night", asks Ivan Ivanevich, "what's that?"

"Who knows?", replies the policeman, "but we have a message at headquarters . . . The message says that when a big party of 2,500 or more Canadians visit a foreign city, they act as if it was Grey Cup night."

The policeman steps back into the shadows and lights a cigarette. "I know one thing", he says, "this is the third night in succession that they have been acting like this. They stand in the streets, looking up at the hotel windows and they shout, "What do you know, Joe?" . . . Joe never leans out his window to answer them. Then, about four o'clock in the morning, they'll all get tired and they go back into the hotel, to their own rooms . . ."

"They came here with their hockey team, didn't they?"

"Right", the policeman replies . . .

"What will go on if the Canutskis happen to win tonight's game . . .?"

Jim Coleman, Southam Press

Those Charming Robots

The fraternal order of goaltenders knows no boundaries when it comes to exchanging classified information on the guys who propel pucks at them — not even from the curtain.

Russian goalie Vladislav Tretiak told reporters that Jacques Plante sat down with him in Montreal before the series began and gave him a "book" on the NHL All-Stars. "Jacques explained the peculiarities of the various NHL players' shots," said Tretiak. "It helped me very much."

This might at least partially explain the way Tretiak has been able to confound hockey experts with his goaltending brilliance in the first three games of the Canada-Russia series. Even those who saw him perform at Sapporo where the Russians won the 1972 Olympics, are astonished how much he has improved.

And based on what he said, the uncanny way he seems to anticipate *Team Canada* shots with his cobra-like glove hand, might well be based on inside knowledge of the various players' shooting tendencies.

Plante's association with Tretiak goes back three years, when he worked with the Russian goalie on his last visit

here. Plante and veteran Russian goalie, Viktor Konovalenko, are Tretiak's idols. Is it dirty pool for Plante to provide Tretiak with such information? Not if you're a member of the goaltenders' lodge, it isn't.

Reporters caught Tretiak after the Russian practice yesterday as he lugged his heavy equipment bag out to the waiting bus. All Russian players pack and carry their own equipment, tape their own sticks, and sharpen their own skates. Assistant-coach Boris Kulagin explained: "It's just like in the parachute corps where a man likes to pack his own parachute."

Tretiak is a lieutenant in the Russian army, prompting one reporter to ask how much money he was paid.

"The same amount as other lieutenants," said Kulagin.

"Did you know that Brad Park makes $200,000 a year?" another reporter asked.

"But Park is a professional," said Kulagin. "Tretiak is only an amateur."

Asked about the calibre of Canadian shooters, Tretiak singled out Phil Esposito as the most dangerous around the net — hardly a surprise to anyone — but also said that Russia's Anatoli Firsov can shoot with the best of the Canadians.

Asked what his duties were in the army, Tretiak said:

"I am in charge of a platoon of eight . . . goaltenders. I teach them goaltending. I'm a graduate of the Institute for Sports, and I'm still attending classes at a special college for physical culture."

It was quite an experience, flying west to Vancouver with the Russians and observing them in total relaxation from a vantage point scant feet away.

You immediately suspected some of them could speak English, by the way they studiously leafed through magazine after magazine, pausing for long periods over each page.

I peeked over one player's shoulder and saw that he had ripped out a magazine page, showing an ultra-modern house full of furniture. And he was writing a note on it, addressed to someone back home, giving them a glimpse of the way some of us live over here. It was a touching moment, watching him grope for the right words to put on the paper.

The players talked and laughed and played cards and moved leisurely about the cabin much like the Expos or any other travelling team. And being young, virile specimens, their eyes lingered longingly over the pretty stewardesses. Air Canada had put aboard Russian-speaking stewardesses, and all the flight announcements were made in Russian. After being served one of the all-time outstanding airline meals, many of the players drifted off to sleep.

But they awoke with considerable excitement when it was announced that they'd be making a brief stop in Edmonton where the mayor and other civic dignitaries were waiting to present them with ten-gallon hats. Since the Russian players are rabid western movie buffs, they couldn't wait to try on their first stetson. Unfortunately, when they filed off the plane, all they were given — besides a series of clammy handshakes — was a crummy little envelope containing a tourist pamphlet you can find in any hotel lobby, and a 19-cent ball-point, left over from Edmonton's summer Klondike Days bash.

They filed back on board grumbling, and Air Canada liaison man Aggie Kukolowicz — who has done an outstanding job of helping make their travels function smoothly — tried to appease them by announcing that he would try to have some cowboy hats flown in from Calgary.

As the jet reved up its engines and slowly taxied away from the line of civic dignitaries, who were standing on the tarmac trying to hold their hands over their ears to ward off the noise and wave goodbye at the same time, one member of the travelling party couldn't resist showing his disappointment with what is commonly known as a gesture of disbelief.

He held up a fist, then extended the two outside fingers to transmit a message which needed no interpretation.

As the plane soared over the Rockies, other passengers began to drift back and mingle with the Russians, asking them for autographs. The players all made a big fuss over a four-year-old girl, as she trundled down the aisle with her mother.

They were at ease, laughing, and obviously thoroughly enjoying this rare moment away from the rink and the curious hordes. Don't ever let anyone tell you Russian hockey players are grim-faced robots. They struck me as model young men you'd be proud to know.

John Robertson, The Montreal Star

A Lifetime of Learning

Professional hockey's top pros confess to confusion in their confrontation with the non-professionals of the Soviet Union. They fail to understand, for example, why their power play, which seldom backfires in the NHL, has averaged one short-handed goal per game in Canada for the comrades.

How does Vladislav Tretiak, allegedly a mediocre goaler, develop the speed of a cobra with his hands? Tretiak, himself, says it's easy. He throws tennis balls, two at a time, against a wall, at close range and grabs them on the rebound.

Then there is the questionnaire which Viacheslav Starshinov, honored USSR sport master, has submitted to members of *Team Canada*. Starshinov claims he will use the information in composing a thesis for his doctorate. The

Canadians wonder whether Viacheslav isn't attempting to make them even more bewildered than they appear to be when they are playing six men against the Soviet five.

"On paper, it looks a lot hazier than it actually is," Ken Dryden, goalie and budding attorney, assured teammates Pat Stapleton and Bill White, as he studied Starshinov's document during breakfast. "Now, here's a toughie," Dryden conceded. "He wants to know to what extent your attitude to people is influenced by feelings of thanks shown for your person by the spectators, gratitude for measures which were put in your sport training, anger against accepted moral inter-relations. There's a lot more. You are asked to answer by underlining one of five digits. Let's say you underline 5. That means an intense sense of responsibility. The figure 3 means it's only so-so. I'd like time to give this more thought."

Stapleton, looking at White, observed: "Geez, Bill, do you suppose Starshinov doesn't realize we're defencemen?"

"The problem of objective tests such as this," Dryden warned them, "is that you wind up saying something you don't mean. You get five choices. Not one of the five may express your attitude."

"I'm in favor of filling one out anyway," White volunteered. "Maybe he doesn't care how I feel. He hasn't sent me a questionnaire yet."

Phil Esposito, whom the Soviets fear, because of his persistence in the slot, and whom they admire because of his unfailing good nature, offered his services gladly. Starshinov would have the benefit of his thoughts and reflections, Phil assured. "The way I see it is this," Phil pontificated, "here's a guy who has spent 26 years going to school. Right? (Starshinov is 32). If there is anything we can do to help him get what he's after, I think we should do it. Right?"

Okay, Phil, here is part of Question 4: "In what extent is your understanding of moral responsibility before society influenced by moral traditions of your social economic society?

Phil excused himself to participate in a responsibility to Mr. Harry Sinden, whose demands are much more immediate than Starshinov's doctorate.

Sinden himself wants to co-operate with Starshinov. It would add dignity to the sport to have Dr. Starshinov listed on the program, in case the comrades come this way again. Certainly, there are several million natives who hope they will be back.

"The trouble I see with Starshinov's questionnaire," Sinden reported, after studying it on the plane from Winnipeg, "is that something was lost in translation. Maybe we should draft a questionnaire for him."

Question 1, Section A would be: "How much of your success do you attribute to our power play?"

Milt Dunnell, The Toronto Star

GAME FIVE

That Losing Streak Has Moscow Smiling

Have you ever seen a political biggie grinning from earlobe to earlobe when he isn't running up and down the Steppes looking for votes?

Well, come back with me to the 14:46 mark of the third period. By now, most of you — and me — have chewed up a knuckle or two, because what had been the laugher for two and a half periods now had become a life and death struggle. Life and death? The hangman was reaching with an itchy finger for the lever that springs the trap door!

You know what had happened up to that point. *Team Canada* had held 3-0 and 4-1 leads. Then rigor mortis set in, and suddenly it was 4-4 and people in *Team Canada* sweaters were falling over themselves trying to get out of the way. Anyway, a couple of seconds before the 14:46 mark, Bobby Clark is against the boards trying to control a bouncing puck. He gets a little wood on it and sends it back to Rod Seiling.

"It was a bad play," Clarke was to mention much later, "a bad play. Ahhhh . . . what guy in his right mind passes the puck back to somebody deep in his own zone at that stage of the game?"

The bouncing puck never did get to Seiling. Or if it did, Seiling was unable to handle it. "I think," said Clarke, "it never got to him."

Anyway, there's a clash of bodies and Valery Kharlamov gets the puck to his linemate, Vladimir Ivanovich Vikulov. From there, it's Soviet puck-handling at its finest. He cuts across the front of the nets, takes Tony Esposito for a cup of coffee in several languages, and slashes the puck into the net.

And in the VIP box at centre ice, the general secretary of the Communist Party is smiling from here to there, and so is Nikolai Podgorny, who is merely the President of the Soviet Union. And so are Alexei Kosygin, who is the prime minister, and Dmitri Polyanski, who is the first deputy prime minister.

Who can blame them? Not me. Not any of the wildly enthusiastic 2,500 Canadian fans in the rink. Surely not the Soviet fans. Not anybody.

Unbelieveable, that's what it was.

"Tell me," George Imlach was asking, "when was the last time you saw . . . no, let me put it this way, how many times does a National Hockey League team go into the final 10 minutes of a game leading 4-1 and lose it 5-4? They've got to give him some help! They can't do things like backing in the way they did.

"Never mind about forecheckers. What any team needs is backcheckers. You don't have a backchecker, and you're in big trouble. A lot of guys worked hard, but 3-0 . . . 4-1 . . . I don't believe it!"

It is probably an accurate assessment of what happened.

Look . . . for two periods — no . . . two and a half periods, you could feel the superiority of *Team Canada*. Take away the first eight minutes of the game, when Tony Esposito (that's the man Imlach was talking about) produced several excellent saves, and it was no contest. Forecheck . . . backcheck . . . people standing up at the blueline and breaking up the Soviets right there!

"You can't let 'em get inside the blueline," Imlach was saying. "You stand up. You stop them up at the blueline. You break up their plays."

That's what the Canadians were doing during the first two and a half periods. And while they were standing up there and breaking up plays and unsettling the Soviets, goals were being scored. Gilbert Perreault throws a delightful head fake at Viktor Kuzkin, then drops a pass back into the slot to Jean-Paul Parisé, and the low shot beats Vladislav Tretiak easily.

That's only part of it, though. Paul Henderson was in alone earlier in the period, and couldn't get away a shot. Frank Mahovlich separated Kuzkin from the puck, came in alone from the side, and was beaten. A good stop on Guy Lapointe . . . and finally, goal! It's only the beginning. It's only in the third minute of the second period, and Bobby Clarke has a goal — assisted by Henderson. Then, later in the period, Henderson has a goal, and in the VIP box our distinguished friends from the Politburo aren't finding too much to smile about. Canada's Arthur Laing likes it a lot.

"At the end of the second period," Henderson was to mention, "they (the Soviets) should have been in Siberia — not on the ice. We had them. Did we run out of gas? I don't think so. I felt good. How about you Bobby?"

Clarke looks at Henderson, grimaces, throws back his head and sighs: "Look . . . we're not a defensive team. Our line (Clarke, Henderson and Ron Ellis) is a defensive line, I suppose, but the team isn't. I'm not blaming anybody, but what I couldn't understand was that for an offensive team, we sure seemed to fall into a defensive shell. Maybe not a shell . . . but we fell back. Nobody told us to do it. I guess we started figuring, well . . . we're leading by three goals, so let's win this game. Dammit. What happened?"

Yuri Blinov scores a goal at 3:34. No panic. Especially since Henderson, who had damaged his neck with a nasty fall late in the second period (he's wearing a collar today) is back and gets the goal back less than a minute later. The fans go wild. Everybody is hugging each other. Arthur Laing is smiling, and Leonid Brezhnev looks glum.

What happened was what Imlach was talking about and what Jean Beliveau was talking about and what a lot of the players on *Team Canada* were talking about.

Vyacheslav Anisin has his back to Esposito — and deflects a shot from the blueline into the net. Eight seconds later Vladimir Shadrin gets another, and now it's 4-3. Two goals in eight seconds, and the laughter is starting to become a nightmare. It is a nightmare. Teams aren't supposed to lose leads that quickly. Goaltenders who have played so well for three quarters of the game don't deserve to get beaten like that.

But there's more to come. Alexander Gusev streaks a shot that seems to hit a Soviet player in front of the net and deflects upward beyond Esposito at 11:31, and now it's 4-4. Then the Clarke pass . . . the bouncing puck . . . Vikulov . . . and smiles all around, starting with the general secretary of the Communist Party. It's smiles from the Soviets — and deservedly so — and a cloud of gloom settles over the Canadian contingent . . . and the players and no doubt, the folks at home.

"Do you know what it reminded me of?" Phil Esposito was asking a few of the curious. "I have to go back to that Canadiens-Boston game when we're leading 5-1 in the second period of a playoff game and Tommy Johnson tells us to cool it. You don't ask the Boston Bruins to cool it when you're leading by four goals. You know what happened? They get six straight goals and we lose the game 7-5 and right there, I suppose, we lose the *Stanley Cup*.

"Now Harry didn't tell us anything. He didn't say to cool it, so I guess it was all our own idea. I don't think . . . no, we didn't run out of gas. We just gave it away."

"When you allow a team to score five goals in one period," Tony Esposito was to say, "there aren't any excuses. Look . . . this is *Stanley Cup* play, and when you've got the big chips going, you've got to come up with the big save. I didn't come up with the big saves. I just blew it, I guess."

Tony Esposito did not make the big saves in the third period, but if it were not for Tony Esposito, *Team Canada* would have trailed the Soviets by several goals in the first period. What happened to *Team Canada* is something that has happened to a lot of hockey teams who encounter superior opposition. It's not conditioning any more, folks. It's not dates. The Soviets lose their composure now and then when they're behind, but they don't become hopelessly disorganized.

They're major leaguers as players and conduct themselves as cool and poised professionals when they're losing a hockey game, which they surely were doing, until nearly midway through the third period.

Team Canada played as well as they could for 50 minutes. They tried as hard as they could. Disappointing? Sure.

Heartbreaking, of course. But when a team tries as hard as this team did last night, two things must be done. You acknowledge their determination and hard work. And then you salute the winners for a remarkable display of professionalism, if you'll pardon the expression, in the face of adversity.

There were a lot of hockey players who conducted themselves admirably. The Clarke-Ellis-Henderson line once again was marvellous.

Yvan Cournoyer still isn't sharp enough to provide the team with the goals they expect of him. Even in the last few seconds, he had a goal on the end of his stick, but was outfoxed by Tretiak on a night the Soviet goalie was ready to be taken.

Frank Mahovlich has had better nights, and some of the other forwards still are far from the level of productivity they bring into the NHL each season.

But the defence remains the weakest part of *Team Canada*. Pat Stapleton and Bill White, I thought, were as steady as usual. Guy Lapointe played well, but when is Brad Park going to demonstrate that all of us didn't have our pockets picked when we felt that he would take over the leadership role in this team? This team won't win unless Park plays a lot better. Time is running out.

I don't like what happened here last night. I don't like it because *Team Canada* lost a game it should have won. Let Leonid Brezhnev smile happily because his system has produced a marvellous group of hockey players, but I don't like the curtain of gloom that enfolded all of the Canadians in this rink.

Give the Soviets supreme credit for an astonishing comeback, but don't ask me to enjoy the sight of two ladies with Canada buttons on their blouses biting their lips to hold back the tears . . . and losing the small skirmish. I don't like to think what other losses in the three remaining games in the series will do to the people here and back home. Especially with Phil Esposito's post-game words still ringing in my ears: "Do I think losing this game will hurt us psychologically in the next game?" he was asking. "It's nothing psychological," he grunted.

"We know now who's the better team!"
Red Fisher, The Montreal Star

Like a Stage Play

It is the middle of the night and Harry Sinden is down. He has bypassed a big press conference at the Lenin Palace of Sport, but now he's here in a hotel suite with the Canadian contingent trying to rationalize yet another defeat.

Midnight or not, it still comes out five to four for the other guys.

Since *Team Canada* first struck Stockholm a week ago, coach Sinden has tried to answer all questions thoroughly and honestly. He is a guy with a face that reflects his feelings. And now his dismay fills the room.

He won't accept the obvious "out" that since his team blew a 4-1 lead in the third period they were beaten by better conditioning, reluctant to get into the philosophical differences between East and West.

The point has been made frequently that NHL players are not conditioned to play under *Stanley Cup* pressure in September, that the fat of summer is still hanging heavy under their money-belts.

"The mistakes we're making don't belong on the calendar," Sinden says. "I haven't seen anything that would make me say anything would be different next month or the month later. They play this game as though there were no scoreboard, no ups and downs," he says of the Russians. "We don't. No team in the NHL would have played the way they did in the last 10 minutes, down 4-1 and still skating and shooting and passing the puck the same way they did in the first period."

The Russions have now won three games and tied one in the eight-game series. The Canadians have won one game.

With the Russians, Sinden believes, it's like a stage play. There are certain things to be done before the curtain comes down and they simply do them without a sense of emotion or concern for peripheral pressures.

Sinden is convinced that Canadians have better individual skills when they are at emotional peaks. But they have letdowns, too; moments of resting on temporary achievements that never seem to penetrate the Russian approach to the game.

He accepts the analogy of Iron Mike, the mechanical baseball pitcher, a machine impervious to time and place and circumstance.

"They never let up," Sinden says, shaking his head, "they keep coming at you."

But it's not his feeling, surprisingly, that the Russians have improved their mechanical skills since he first saw them 12 years ago at Stockholm, when he played for the Whitby Dunlops in a world tournament. The change over the years has been Canada's, a dozen years of barely perceptible decline.

"From 1958, when I played against them, until tonight I've seen no great progress in the Russian team," he said. "Some sure, but not that much. I think we've slipped — either stood still or slipped back. And they've caught us."

Trent Frayne, The Toronto Star

The Taller They Stand

Phil Esposito waved to the world from his backside on opening night in Moscow . . . a monumental pratfall that couldn't have happened to a more undeserving fellow. As the big guys fall with loud thuds — Vic Hadfield, Brad Park et al — the towering Paisano should never be seen as anything but a man standing tall.

"Damn flowers," Esposito said as he patiently signed autographs for Russian youngsters outside the rink while his teammates fled to the sanctuary of the bus. "Nice kids, the ones who skated out and gave us them. But the flowers, the stem fell off. I stepped right on it and was on my ass in a flash.

"Must have looked good, huh? A hundred million guys watching all around the world, brass bands playing, the Russian cats in the stands, and here am I dumped on the ice. So I waved to the folks back home in the Soo, a wave from the dummy with egg on his face."

The Soo, of course, is Sault Ste. Marie where the Brothers Esposito are the Italian-Canadians of most note. If you don't believe that, you should have been along with me for the cab ride from the rink yesterday. Phil read out each name on a 300-name telegram to his brother, Tony. It sounded like the Palermo 'phone book.

"Hey, Tony, listen to these. Luigi Bertolli . . . hey, the Frank Corsa trio . . . the guys at Angie Petrella's furniture store . . . Mr. and Mrs. Frank Donatelli — Hey, I didn't know Frank got married . . . Guiseppe Berretta; boy I used to whip him in street fights . . ."

Esposito has been doing it all in this series. Reading wires and letters the others throw away unopened, signing autographs for strangers some others ignore, jabbing teammates who need the jab, making plays that keep Canada close.

"C'mon guys," he shouted in a pre-game warmup at Stockholm. "Either start playing this game or get the . . . home."

Three players took him literally, including Vic Hadfield. When the chips were down and Harry Sinden needed every last soul behind him—whether to play or to round out a complement for vital practices — the captain of the New York Rangers "got the . . . home." His own NHL teammates shuddered.

"Now you still wonder why we beat those bastards every year?" Frosty Forrestall, the Bruins' trainer, wondered in his Boston accent. "Take a look at the captain of New York going home because he can't win a place on the team."

Don Awrey, with wounded pride, and Wayne Cashman, with an injured mouth, may have wanted to accompany Hadfield. But not as long as Bobby Orr and Phil Esposito are around. They're leaders and they command respect . . . rather, obedience . . . from those who willingly follow.

There's one incontestable fact emerging from this spectacle — Phil Esposito is some helluva hockey player. Rough around the edges to be sure, but an engaging soul and a fierce competitor. We've learned much about hockey in the past month, and the growing stature of Phil Esposito is not the least of our discoveries.

Ted Blackman, The Gazette, Montreal

GAME SIX

Beating the System and Winning the Match

Harry Sinden was wearing a light suit and a dark frown. He cleared his throat . . . worked his jaws, and said: "The refereeing was incompetent."

Officials produced by Bunny Ahearne (president of the International Ice Hockey Federation), the two Sinden called the most incompetent officials he had seen in his career, did not help the Canadians win Game Six; Franz Baader and Joseph Kompalla.

I don't know how they rate alongside Art Skov and Bruce Hood, but unless I'm sadly mistaken, I've heard coaches—including Sinden—talk the same way about referees in the National Hockey League. The only major difference is that the monologue usually takes place after a losing game.

The refereeing was bad—but only in one major area. It was bad in the matter of calling off-sides, and for this, I blame the system and not the men. Three men always should be in a position to call a game better than two. But in the matter of calling penalties, there wasn't much to growl about. Not much at all.

When Gary Bergman whips a man's feet from under him, that's a penalty. And when Phil Esposito rushes at a man and carries him into the boards, even Art Skov would call that a charging penalty. And when Phil dumps the man on the way to the penalty box, maybe Skov doesn't call it, but if Joseph Kompalla wants to call it, there's a rule in the book—any book—which says he can.

I thought a slashing penalty to Dennis Hull—what I could see of it—was not a good one, but when Phil Esposito high-sticks a player and draws blood—that's five minutes.

Okay, don't take my word for it. How does John Ferguson's word suit you? After all, wasn't it soft-spoken John who railed at the official repeatedly late in the second period, just about the time Esposito was drawing blood on Rags Ragulin?

"But the off-sides . . . the off-sides," complained Ferguson. "What are we going to about that?"

One thing *Team Canada* can try to do about that is turn thumbscrews down on any further use of the officials in the remaining games. But that's not the area in which *Team Canada* has to concentrate most of its efforts. The penalties . . . that's what hurts and almost sent the team reeling to another defeat. Bad penalties.

It's not as if Harry and John don't know better. They have pointed out these things repeatedly, and it's astonishing to me that a man with the stature of an

Esposito, for example, would fall for so many sucker plays.

Who's Phil trying to fool? Who told him that he can do this team any good sitting on his haunches in the penalty box and screaming sour nothings at the officials? Harry can talk about trying to play a game when a team is shorthanded for 17 minutes, including two minutes with the team short two men—but the fact is that this type of refereeing is predictable. It didn't suddenly pop out of Bunny Ahearne's watch pocket. All of it should have been part of the preparation for this series, and if *Team Canada* players continue to go for the sucker plays, they won't be as fortunate as they were last night.

The fact is, all of the *Team Canada* scoring took place within one minute and 23 seconds in the second period, after Yuri Liapkin, an astonishingly proficient defenceman, had provided the Soviets with a 1-0 lead earlier in the period.

The goal which beat Ken Dryden came on a long shot that caught the far corner. But then, four minutes later, Rod Gilbert does some sturdy work in front of the Soviet net, gets away a shot at Vladislav Tretiak, and Dennis Hull is there to lift the rebound over a fallen Tretiak. A little more than a minute later, Red Berenson gets the puck to Yvan Cournoyer and Tretiak is beaten. Fifteen seconds later, Paul Henderson gets away a harmless-looking shot along the ice from a step inside the blueline, and Tretiak gets his living-legend reputation tarnished a little when he allows the puck to skip into the net.

How's that, comrades?

Ready to quit?

Who's kidding who? Know what happens after that? *Team Canada's* offence goes ph-t-t-t, largely because they're forced into a position where they have to kill off penalties. Forced by themselves, that is. First. It's Hull with his slashing penalty, and that man Alexander Yakushev gets a goal nine seconds after Hull is sitting on his britches. Then assistant coach John Ferguson gets his bench penalty, while over on the other side of the rink, Espo is drawing blood on Ragulin.

Get the picture?

Now, let me tell you a little bit about what kept *Team Canada* alive and well with its 3-2 lead through the agonizing moments when the team was short-handed two men, and during the remaining three minutes on Esposito's silly penalty and during the minor earned by Ron Ellis with a breath over two minutes remaining in the game. Let me tell you something about what it was that kept *Team Canada* with its head well above water, even though the team trails the series 3-2 with only two games remaining.

It starts with Ken Dryden. Remember the guy who was mentioning the other day that he felt he was the odd man out, and deservedly so? Remember the goalie who was thrashed for 12 goals in two previous appearances

against the Soviets? Well, it seems that Dryden has been working extremely well in practices lately. "He was very, very sharp in practice," Ferguson was mentioning last night, "and don't forget he's still one of the best goaltenders in the world. Isn't he?"

Dryden is among the best goaltenders in the world, but not in this series. Not up until last night, at any rate. And in the moments leading up to Game Six the triple-guessing among people who don't really have a stake in any of the decisions was as loud as a Soviet taxi driver haggling with a tourist over the price of a trip through Moscow streets.

How could Harry do this thing? He decided to throw in the babushka as far as the series was concerned? Who's helping him make up his mind? Vsevolod Bobrov? Why did he decide to change Tony Esposito? After all, what did Tony do wrong aside from getting beaten for five goals the other night? What about poor, old E. J.? Doesn't Eddie Johnston deserve the chance to get his name in Tass, Pravda and Sovietski Sports?

Hold on to that genius lapel pin for another few days, Harry. It's worth at least three sticks of bubble gum. Maybe four. Harry's choice of Dryden was right on the Soviet button. Dryden killed the Soviets with numerous big saves, including one he made in the second period while his stick was seven feet away. And how about the one he took away from Kharlamov while our side was short two men?

Know something? That's really Brad Park playing on defence—not Bob Blackburn. The guy was knocking people on their ahems last night. He also was managing to find people with passes who wore the same sweater he does.

Bill White and Pat Stapleton can play on my team any time.

Guy Lapointe was just fine. Aggressive. Tough. Carried the puck well.

And now . . . about this kid Serge Savard! Remember the defenceman who was knocking them dead a few years ago? Remember the guy who won the *Conn Smythe Trophy*? He's back again. All the way. Any guy who came to Europe with a cracked ankle, stayed out of action for ten days, and then could play as Serge did last night—mark him down as high-quality stuff. Even with his spin-around, he's grade A. He was also a life-saver last night.

If you're starting to get the idea that I thought defence won it for *Team Canada*—which I now refuse to call Cream Canada—you're right:

The entire defence corps—hey, did I forget to mention Gary Bergman—was superb. The penalty-killers . . . Peter Mahovlich, Red Berenson, Ron Ellis . . . were exceptional at times, and when the Big Red Machine managed to slip through, Dryden was there.

I'm glad for Dryden. The guy has been simply too great

during his brief career with the Canadiens to come out of this series with a black eye, which is surely what he had developed the two times he played in the series. "Ken who?" people were asking since Game Four.

The anvil (aimed at Dryden's temple) chorus had reached a crescendo in recent days, so it's good that he produced as well as he did. Very good—for *Team Canada* and for Dryden.

It's good that the entire defence corps—particularly Park—played so well, because confusion and indecision have played alongside too many of them in too many games.

It appears that ex-Cream Canada finally is starting to demonstrate why it is that NHL calibre play has been accepted as the best there is. The Soviets have been superb. It is no small achievement to beat a team of the Soviet calibre while playing nearly one-third of the game short-handed.

It's true that the Soviets interfere frequently, but that's why the Baaders and Kompallas are there. If they don't call the interference, they're not calling it for both sides, and since this is so, what gives *Team Canada* the right to react with stupid penalties? Does the word "stupid" make the hairs on the nape of your neck bristle? Sorry about that, chaps. The exercise is to win, and it's tough enough

beating the Soviets at even strength. Do you see what I'm getting at, Harry?

It's all right for you, Harry, to pull at the lapel of your light suit and frown darkly—again—and say:

"I am very, very concerned that the two referees who worked tonight may work again. I think a meeting is in order at this time to see that they don't work again in this series."

It is also all right to say: "a lot of times during a game you become frustrated, so you react."

And hey, there, Bobby Orr! It's all right to say: "Phil (Esposito) got a double minor and I haven't figured it out yet. I want to know how the hell we're supposed to play our game. It's a damn shame they won't let us play our game. Whatever Phil did, I'm behind him 100 per cent!"

All of these things are all right to say, but on the ice is the place where the game is played. Stay there, and you're good enough to win the remaining two games and the series. Take as many penalties as you did last night, and it's almost too much to ask for the defensive team to do it again.

Y'hear?????

Red Fisher, *The Montreal Star*

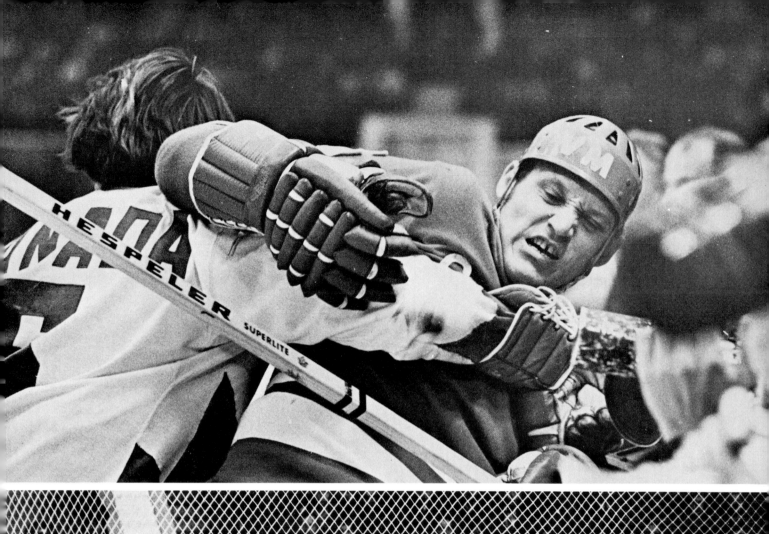

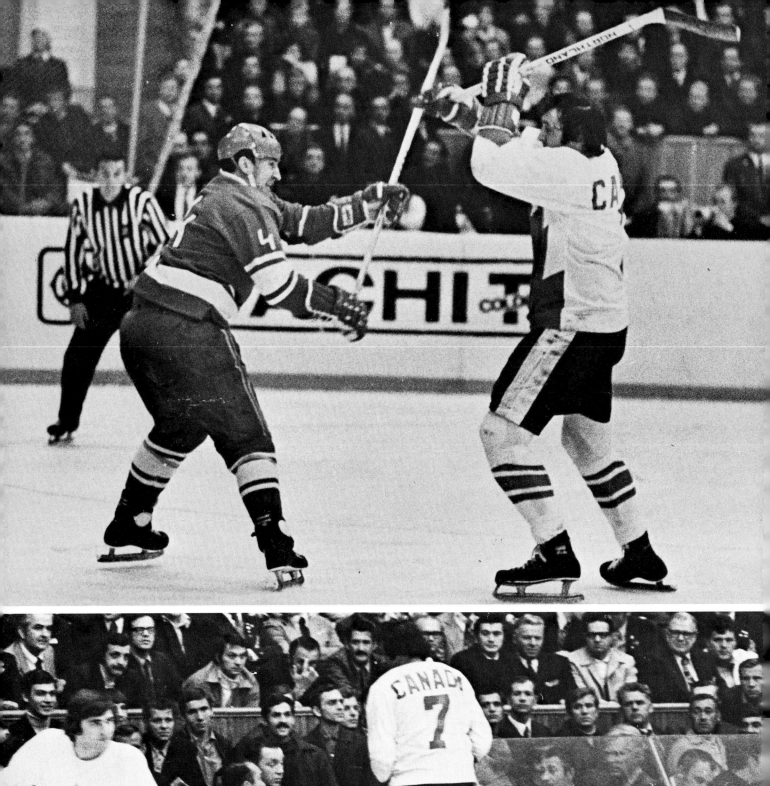

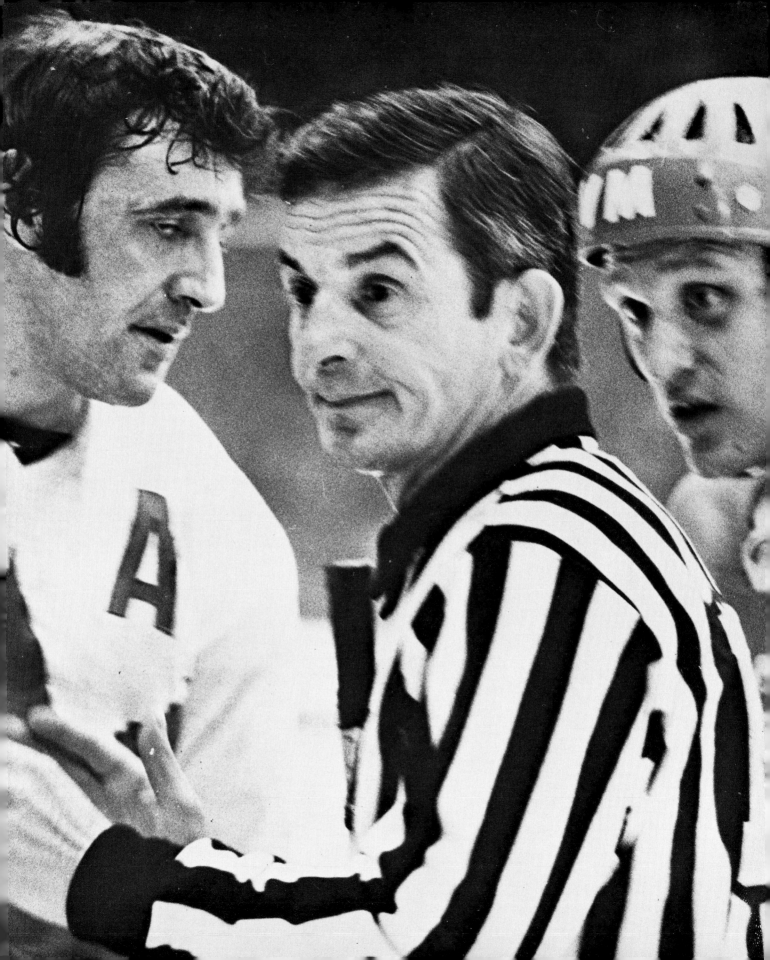

GAME SEVEN

This One a Steal

Come back with me to Stockholm . . . oh, about 10 days ago. Harold Ballard, who is the owner of Toronto Maple Leafs — courtesy of a $7 million bank loan — is sitting on a rubbing table outside the *Team Canada* dressing room. The players come off the ice, and as Phil Esposito passes Ballard, he says: "Harold, I've just been talking with Paul (Henderson) and Ron (Ellis)."

"Yeah?" asks Ballard.

"Know the first thing they say they're gonna do when they get back home?"

"Tell me," says Ballard.

"They're gonna ask for a lot more money."

"Har-umph," grunts Ballard.

You should know that a couple . . . maybe three months ago, Henderson and Ellis signed contracts with Toronto Maple Leafs. They're not kidding about wanting more money even before they start collecting on it.

Mark me down as a guy who wouldn't walk from here to there to renegotiate a contract. When was the last time a player returned part of his paycheque when he had a lousy season? There have been extenuating circumstances between seasons for those players who are on long-term contracts. The World Hockey Association has spiralled salaries into areas beyond all reason, so if I were an owner and one of my big people was on a long-term contract, I'd come back to him and toss a few more dollars into his jeans. Didn't the Rangers do it with Jean Ratelle? Canadiens, maybe, with Yvan Cournoyer?

But I draw the line at renegotiating contracts which were signed since the end of last season — until Henderson put in the winning goal at 17:54 of the final period. When Paul's goal went in to provide Canada with a 4-3 triumph and an even split of the series, all the rules touching on morality went thataway. Particularly, friends, since it isn't my money.

What I am saying is: Do it, Harold. Give the guy what he wants. Go to the jolly bank manager and stick him for a few more dollars, if necessary, but do it. Crack open your son Bill's piggy bank, but get the dough somewhere. Sell old pictures of Vic Hadfield on a dartboard. Have a Paul Henderson Night at Maple Leaf Gardens. Sell apples door to door. Give him the hot dogs concession . . . anything. But let him know right now he's got the dough, because have you got any idea what his winning goal in what surely appeared to be a losing cause — or a tie, at best — is worth?

Alongside it, the crown jewels of the non-czar are

five-and-dime stuff. The *Stanley Cup* is a shaving mug. Your Rolls-Royce is a Stanley Steamer. That goal made Phyllis Diller beautiful. Ma Kettle a sexpot. Frank Sinatra a heavyweight boxing champion and Boris Karloff, an author of fairy tales. It brought everybody from way down here, to way UP there, and that's got to be worth something.

Okay . . . who's the first one to nominate Paul Henderson for Prime Minister? Or at least, a member of the Cabinet?

"Of all the goals I've ever scored," Henderson was saying last night, "this one gave me the most satisfaction."

It's not difficult to imagine.

Lookit, I don't know how you saw this game, but as far as I was concerned, the outcome made the Brinks job look like a purse snatch. There are several noteworthy people who don't agree with me, starting with the coach of the team, Harry Sinden, but in the delicate dialogue of hockey, this one was a steal.

"I thought," he said, "that we played our best game when they had the puck. What I mean is . . . we positioned ourselves better than in any of the other games. We weren't so hot when we had the puck."

Okay, Harry. But it was still a Brinks job, and they do happen in hockey games. It makes up for the *Team Canada* 5-4 loss last Friday after our side held a 4-1 lead with a little more than 10 minutes remaining. It would have been nice to win that one, but sit back and breathe a huge s-i-g-hhhhh of relief to come out of last night with better than a tie.

Let's go back to the beginning. All of you who have made this Canada-Soviet series the biggest (the latest ratings say double) television attraction in Canadian history, must have seen Phil Esposito open the scoring in the fifth minute of the game, nine seconds after Eugeni Mishakov returned to the ice after completing a penalty. It was Esposito stuff from start to finish. In the slot . . . about 20 feet in front of Vlady Tretiak . . . a low shot.

And then you must have seen Brad Park out to lunch shortly after the midway mark of the period, and Alex Yakushev tying the score. How about Vladimir Petrov at 16:27, while Bill White was in the penalty box? The Yakushev goal was not a good one: a 40-footer through Tony Esposito's legs. The Petrov goal was another case of the Soviet forward taking the goalie for a cup of vodka. Big trouble at this point. Very big trouble.

Esposito was shaky and the Soviets were turning it on. They appeared to be doing faily well what they pleased, and the wonder of it was that *Team Canada* came out of the first period with the score deadlocked.

Esposito again — helped immeasurably by Serge Savard. The big Canadiens' defenceman is the last man back at the Soviet blueline. He makes his spin-around play, gets away with it, and feeds Jean-Paul Parisé. Then its over to Esposito in the slot. The time was 17:34.

Know how I felt going into the second period? To put it bluntly, the word is pessimistic. Esposito, the goalie, is shaky. *Team Canada*, as a group, isn't getting the chances at Tretiak, mostly because the Soviet defencemen are laying on the muscle, and hey! Forget all that stuff about the Soviets being reluctant to use their bodies. At times they must have made John Ferguson feel like J. C. Tremblay.

It wasn't good, but what did Tony Esposito do during the between-period hiatus? Who pumped steel into his biceps? He made old men feel young again. Without Esposito, it's curtains. As Sinden said, perhaps *Team Canada* people positioned themselves well, and if that's so, it was probably for a parade. The Soviets pummelled Esposito, they outshot *Team Canada* 13-7, and those weren't rubles they were tossing at the Chicago man. If you're interested, the snow started falling on Moscow streets midway through last night's game — and those weren't snowballs Esposito had to catch.

Mikhailov . . . Liapkin . . . Maltsev . . . Yakushev . . . Lutchenko . . . Vikulov is in alone with 40 seconds remaining, and he shoots wide. Five, maybe six great stops in a period, and *Team Canada* comes out of it still locked up with the Soviets at 2-2. Does that sound like a team playing its best game defensively? There were so many Soviets in the Canadian zone during the second period, Esposito must have thought he was taking the salute at a May Day parade.

It's happened before in hockey games, right? A team dominates (the Soviets outshot *Team Canada* 31-25) for a long spell, but then the breaks go the other way and strange things happen.

What could be stranger than Rod Gilbert taking the puck off the back-boards in the third minute of play in the final period, skating unmolested in front of the net, and then beating Tretiak with a backhander? Soviet defencemen normally don't allow that to happen, but a guy isn't perfect, is he, Vsevolod? That goal was enough to snap the Canadian fans out of their stupor, and maybe . . . just maybe . . . But there's that man Yakushev again at the 5:15 mark, while Gary Bergman is in the penalty box. Maltsev feeds through the crease and Yakushev has his second goal of the night. It's 3-3, and Canadian hearts are fluttering. Even a tie is pretty good at this point.

But hold it. There's more to come. The way the Tass journalists reported it was "uncovered crudity" — an extension, no doubt, of the slash which put Valery Kharlamov out of the game.

This latest smidgen of "naked crudity" occurred with three minutes and 34 seconds remaining in the game and the teams — apparently — heading toward a tie, which could have been almost as good as a loss for *Team Canada*. Any game which erases any hope of winning a series, is as good as a loss, right?

Anyway, the puck is behind Esposito, and Boris Mikhailov, a tough and gritty forward, is scuffling for it with Gary Bergman.

Now let Bergman tell you about it:

"It's the first time I've ever been kicked during a hockey game. The first time . . . two, maybe three times. I've got a welt on my leg where his skate came through the shin pad, and after that, all I wanted was a piece of him. Any part of him would do. I couldn't believe it. 'Is this happening to me?' I said to myself."

Bergman was chuckling about the incident in the moments after the game, but it was no laughing matter when it happened. Bergman fought to get clear of Mikhailov, and then before he could disentangle himself, here comes Yvan Cournoyer, pumping punches at the Soviet forward. Bergman gets clear and throws a punch over the shoulder (a downercut) of Phil Esposito, and now some of the Soviets are coming off the bench and who's there to meet them — also off the bench — but Bill Goldsworthy! He's fouling up the air with the cold stare he levels at the Soviets, but the blade of his stick is aimed at the navel of the Soviet forward nearest him.

By NHL standards, as Sinden was to explain with tongue in cheek later, the third period wasn't rough. It surely wasn't uncovered crudity. But it's the most delicate incident of the series thus far.

Punches were thrown, including several by Mikhailov. That hasn't happened before. Players came off the bench. That, surely, hasn't happened before. The result: major penalties for Bergman and Mikhailov, which is something of a break, since Cournoyer also had a large chunk of the action.

Normally, the brief explosion should have been enough to establish a situation in which both teams would be satisfied to allow the clock to run out. But when a guy's got on eye on a contract that he wants renegotiated, a few minutes can be an eternity.

Once again, it's Savard who starts the play. He passes from his own zone to Henderson, and now the Toronto left-winger is moving in on two Soviet defencemen.

"I tried to push the puck through the legs of one of them," said Henderson, "and I got a bit of a break on it. The puck hits his skate, deflected it to his right, and that gave me the chance I needed. While he was looking for it, I moved around him. I had pretty good balance when I let the shot go. What I mean is, I put it exactly where I wanted the puck to go. Upstairs. The next thing I knew I was flat on my rear, but then I was kinda concerned when the light didn't go on. I looked at the referee, though, and he had his hand up, and say — what a feeling."

Red Fisher, The Montreal Star

GAME EIGHT

A Victory of Sorts

Is it really necessary to mention that when Paul Henderson scored his third straight winning goal to earn *Team Canada* its 6-5 victory and the series, goalie Ken Dryden skated frantically down the ice to join the entire roster which had fallen on Henderson in a helpless, beautiful tangle of love?

Joy . . . pride . . . determination . . . dedication . . .they were part of this night. But how about fear?

It's the 12:56 mark of the third period and the Soviets who had led the game throughout the evening and went into the final period with a two-goal bulge, were not skating in dazed, little circles. They had seen their 5-3 lead whittled to 5-4 by Phil Esposito's second goal of the night at 2:27 of the period. Now there's a scramble in the Soviet goalmouth, and Yvan Cournoyer scores one of the biggest goals of his life, but the red light doesn't go on. The referee has his arm raised to signal the goal, but not everybody sees it. Among them is Eagleson, the players' man.

Eagleson was sitting on a front row seat at centre ice. He stood, leaped straight ahead over a five-foot wall to the floor. In front of him was a wall of Soviet police, and Eagleson bumped into several of them on his way down. One of the police turned and shoved Eagleson. The players' man shoved back.

In an instant, Eagleson was grasped firmly by a half-dozen of the police and was half-pushed, half-dragged to the closest exit.

Even while the Canadian players were flinging their arms around each other over the comeback that had provided them with a tie, with a little over seven minutes remaining, fear started to develop as small pockets of people watched Eagleson struggling helplessly in the iron fists of the Soviet police. Peter Mahovlich was the first player to notice the scuffle. He raced to the boards. Then Gary Bergman was there, flailing at the police. Then the other players on the ice, some of them straddling the boards and tugging at the police.

Now all of the players were over the boards, and so were people like Bill Goldsworthy, who hadn't been dressed for the game. Wayne Cashman was another. Ferguson. Harry Sinden.

Eagleson was snatched away from the police by his players. They freed him and then, white-faced, he was sliding across the ice toward the Canadian bench. If you've ever seen one of your own rescued from a near-panic situation, then you'll know how a lot of us felt at that

moment. He got to the players' bench and shook his fist at the goal judge in a final gesture of defiance, and only then did the lump of fear start to melt. Then a moment later . . .

"Look at the police," somebody said.

They marched into the arena . . . 15 . . . 20 . . . 28 of them . . . and the buzz of fear started again. But they were there, this time, only to serve as a deterrent to any other delicate situations. They took their positions . . . staring straight ahead . . . stone-faced . . . fearsome-looking. And on the other side of the arena, others marched in.

I don't know if this incident had any effect on the players. I suspect it did. They are, after all, human beings. They react to things like this. If they're good enough, as they proved last night, they react to adversity, as they did by coming from behind 1-0, 2-1, 3-2, and 5-3 deficits to win it all, finally, 6-5.

Maybe nobody will ever know. Perhaps the vision of 19 hockey players and others who weren't in the lineup racing to the aid of one of their own in a world and a system apart from home, did something to the Soviets, as well as to *Team Canada*. All that's known for certain is that after two periods of struggling to stay alive, in hockey dialogue, *Team Canada* played as it never has before.

Does a team, which had struggled from behind three times in a hockey game, settle for a tie after heading into the final 20 minutes of play with a two-goal deficit? Look around you, and you'll find plenty of teams more than gratified to leave a game with one-half of the spoils.

Not this one. Have you any idea how difficult it is for a team to outshoot the Soviets 13-5 in a final period?

Relentlessly they came . . . even though they had a tie in their fists. Winning is everything, especially in this series. Skate . . . shoot . . . hit . . . skate some more . . . hit again.

And now the seconds are disappearing, and the Canadians are pressing . . . pressing . . . and can it be? Henderson, who had scored the winning goals in Games Two and Three of this half of the eight-game series, is among a cluster of people in front of Vadlislav Tretiak. He shoots . . . and theres' a rebound. He shoots again . . . the light isn't on, but the players' sticks are raised and Dryden is skating down the ice and the players are spilling over the boards. The lump is there again! The numbness is there! People stand and stare at each other in disbelief. The roars are pouring from their throats . . . loud and high . . . and the flags are waving and strangers lumped into a family by common cause are hugging each other.

It was a night that started badly, and, at times, threatened to get worse. But on and on they came in a game with tension unmatched anywhere.

Actually, the tension had started before the game began. The Soviets apparently had agreed to use the same two referees who had handled Game Three for the final

game. Then there was a change of mind. No, the referees who had allowed Game Two to get out of hand, were the Soviets Choice. There were endless meetings. It reached the level of Senator Arthur Laing and the head of the Soviet Sports Committee — and then it was taken away from them and returned to the hockey people — which is where it should have stayed. At last, after many meetings and amid rumors that the final game would not be played, the compromise was reached. One referee from Game Two; another from Game Three.

So, Game Four is only a couple of minutes old, when Bill White is caught tripping. Then, Pete Mahovlich follows him into the box, and that remarkably accomplished Soviet forward, Alexander Yakushev, scores.

The elbows and sticks are high. Emotions are raging. Vladimir Petrov is penalized at 3:44, and a little more than a minute later, with Mahovlich and Petrov in the penalty box, Jean-Paul Parisé is called for interference, the first of five straight interference calls to be made in the first period. (In preceding games, coach Harry Sinden had railed about the lack of interference calls.)

Parisé objects to the call. As he was to explain later:

"Call it holding. Call it anything you want, but how can you interfere with a man when he has the puck? Then he (West German referee Joseph Kompalla) gives me a misconduct, and that's as much as I can take. I guess it was stupid . . ."

Parisé ran at Kompalla with his stick raised. He made a threatening gesture at the referee and repeated it — and now Parisé was out of the game. The players milled around the referee, their voices raised in anger.

A chair comes spilling out over the boards from the Canadian bench and slides across the ice. Another follows.

The crowd rises and chants: "Let's go home, let's go home!"

That was the first time during the evening the players' man, Eagleson, left his seat. This time, he took the orderly, objective approach. He walked quickly around the rink to the Canadian bench.

"Cool it," he told the men on the bench. "Tell them to back off," he told Sinden.

Team Canada recovered from its brief moment of irrationalism, and suddenly things started to fall into the proper squares. The Soviets are shorthanded, and Esposito swipes at a puck in the slot, which is a rebound of a Brad Park shot, and the score is tied. Ron Ellis is penalized, and Vladimir Lutchenko streaks a shot from a step inside the blueline for another go-ahead goal. In the 17th minute of play, Jean Ratelle and Park are at it . . . Ratelle feeds to Park and the defenceman lofts a short shot beyond Tretiak.

The teams traded goals in the first half of the second period, with Vladimir Shadrin scoring after only 21 seconds when the puck flew high and far off the mesh behind the nets, and Bill White scored from close in at the 10:32 mark. Then, perhaps one of the finest saves of the games when Dryden stops Boris Mikhailov, followed four seconds later by the game's lowest point.

How many times have you seen Phil Esposito lose an important faceoff? And stand there in dismay while a go-ahead goal goes in?

Only four seconds elapse between the brilliant stop on Mikhailov and the goal by Yakushev. The faceoff takes place to Dryden's left, Shadrin sweeps the puck toward the goalmouth, even while Cournoyer is breaking for the blueline, and Yakushev snaps it along the ice beyond Dryden. If there was one moment in this hockey game when some of the *Team Canada* players were upset and in disarray — I said, "If" — that was it. Esposito was still in the faceoff circle staring numbly ahead of him. The crowd was stilled. And the hush became even deeper when Valery Vasiliev scored again for the Soviets at the 16:44 mark, while Pat Stapleton was in the penalty box.

Two goals down. The Soviets are skating with wings on their feet. Was this the way it was to finish? Was this the way all of the hard work, the emotional highs and lows . . . the internal strife . . . was this it?

A lot of people thought so. But somebody forgot to tell *Team Canada*.

For the first two periods of the game, Frank Mahovlich — who had not been used in the last two games — was on a line with Esposito and Cournoyer. The results weren't quite as productive as *Team Canada* officials had hoped. Anyway, the first rule in games where a team trails by one or two goals — especially two — is to change the alignments wherever it's felt necessary.

Peter Mahovlich was the left-winger on the line for the third period, and it was Peter who started it all. The same Peter who in the moments before the game stood with a guy looking onto the empty ice and said: "For most of the guys, this thing is bigger than anything. More pressure than the *Stanley Cup*. I'd like to say the same thing, but right now I can't. The biggest pressure for me was two years ago when we won the *Stanley Cup*. First time on a winner, right? A *Stanley Cup* winner. I'd been with a Calder Cup team before, but a *Stanley Cup* — the first one — that's everything, right?

"But I'm hoping for this one. I'm hoping for Frank. A guy who's scored all those goals, and tonight he's going into the game as a penalty-killer. That's good. That's the way to start. He'll be all right."

He looked at the ice and chuckled grimly: "We're better hockey players. The players they're throwing out . . . I don't think any of them would have any trouble finding jobs, but only three or four of them would be invited to the All-Star game. I know this: I've never been interfered

with more . . . had more high sticks . . . spears . . . kicks . . . than I've had in this series. . . ."

Peter brought his thoughts and his hopes for his brother Frank into the game with him. Isn't this what professional sport is all about, when a man who hoped so strongly for someone else finally is the instrument that replaces the object of his high hopes? Was that what aroused Peter so much on his first shift in the third period?

He made all of the play on the goal scored by Esposito. He carried the puck into the area behind the net and to the left of Tretiak, and got it out to Esposito in the slot. Espo swipes at the puck — and misses. Another swipe — and it's 5-4.

The rest you know.

Red Fisher, The Montreal Star

GAME 1 — MONTREAL, SEP. 2, USSR 7, CANADA 3

FIRST PERIOD

1. Canada, P. Esposito (F. Mahovlich, Bergman) 0:30. 2. Canada, Henderson (Clarke) 6:32. 3. USSR, Zimin (Yakushev, Shadrin) 11:40. 4. USSR, Petrov (Mikhailov) 17:28.

Penalties — Henderson, 1:03; Yakushev, 7:04; Mikhailov, 15:11; Ragulin, 17:19.

SECOND PERIOD

5. USSR, Kharlamov (Maltsev) 2:40. 6. USSR, Kharlamov (Maltsev) 10:18.

Penalties — Clarke, 5:16; Lapointe, 12:53.

THIRD PERIOD

7. Canada, Clarke (Ellis, Henderson) 8:32. 8. USSR, Mikhailov (Blinov) 13:32. 9. USSR, Zimin (unassisted) 14:29. 10. USSR, Yakushev (Shadrin) 18:37.

Penalties — Kharlamov, 14:45; Lapointe, 19:41.

GAME 2 — TORONTO, SEP. 4, CANADA 4, USSR 1

FIRST PERIOD

No scoring.
Penalties — Park, 10:08; Henderson, 15:19.

SECOND PERIOD

1. Canada, Esposito (Park, Cashman) 7:14.
Penalties: Gusev, 2:07; Zimin, 4:13; Bergman, 15:16; Liapkin, 19:54 and Kharlamov, 19:54.

THIRD PERIOD

2. Canada, Cournoyer (Park) 1:19. 3. USSR, Yakushev (Liapkin, Zimin) 5:53. 4. Canada, P. Mahovlich (Esposito) 6:47. 5. Canada, F. Mahovlich (Mikita, Cournoyer) 8:59.
Penalties: Clarke, 5:15; Stapleton, 6:14.

GAME 3 — WINNIPEG, SEP. 6, CANADA 4, USSR 4

FIRST PERIOD

1. Canada, Parisé (White, Esposito) 1:54. 2. USSR, Petrov (unassisted) 3:16. 3. Canada, Ratelle (Cournoyer, Bergman) 18:25.
Penalties: Vasiliev, 3:02; Cashman, 8:01; Parisé 15:47.

SECOND PERIOD

4. Canada, Esposito (Cashman, Parisé) 4:19. 5. USSR, Kharlamov (Tsigankov) 12:56. 6. Canada, Henderson (Ellis Clarke) 13:47. 7. USSR, Lebedev (Vasiliev, Anisin) 14:59. 8. USSR, Bodunov (Anisin) 18:28.
Penalties: Petrov, 4:46; Lebedev, 11:00.

THIRD PERIOD

No scoring.
Penalties — White, Mishakov, 1:33; Cashman, 10:44.

GAME 4 — VANCOUVER, SEP. 8, USSR 5, CANADA 3

FIRST PERIOD

1. USSR, Mikhailov (Lutchenko, Petrov) 2:01. 2. USSR, Mikhailov (Lutchenko, Petrov) 7:29.
Penalties — Goldsworthy, 1:24; Goldsworthy, 5:58; Esposito, 19:29.

SECOND PERIOD

3. Canada, Perreault, 5:37. 4. USSR, Blinov (Petrov, Mikhailov) 6:34. 5. USSR, Vikulov (Kharlamov, Maltsev) 13:52.
Penalties — Kuskin, 8:39.

THIRD PERIOD

6. Canada, Goldsworthy (Esposito, Bergman) 6:54. 7. USSR, Shadrin (Yakushev, Vasiliev) 11:05. 8. Canada, Hull (Esposito, Goldsworthy) 19:38.
Penalties — Petrov, 2:01.

GAME 5 — MOSCOW, SEP. 22, USSR 5, CANADA 4

FIRST PERIOD

1. Canada, Parisé (Perreault, Gilbert) 15:30.
Penalties — Ellis, 3:49; Kharlamov, 12:25.

SECOND PERIOD

2. Canada, Clarke (Henderson) 2:36. 3. Canada, Henderson (Lapointe, Clarke) 11:47.
Penalties — Ellis, 5:38; Kharlamov, 5:38; Bergman, 8:13; Blinov, 20:00; White, 20:00.

THIRD PERIOD

4. USSR, Blinov (Petrov, Kuzkin) 3:34. 5. Canada, Henderson (Clarke) 4:56. 6. USSR, Anisin (Liapkin, Yakushev) 9:05. 7. USSR, Shadrin (Anisin) 9:13. 8. USSR, Gusev (Ragulin, Kharlamov) 11:41. 9. USSR, Vikulov (Kharlamov) 14:46.
Penalties — Clarke, 10:25; Tsigankov, 10:25.

GAME 6 — MOSCOW, SEP. 24, CANADA 3, USSR 2

FIRST PERIOD

No scoring.
Penalties — Bergman, 10:21; Esposito, 13:11.

SECOND PERIOD

1. USSR, Liapkin (Yakushev) 1:12. 2. Canada, Hull 5:13. 3. Canada, Cournoyer (Berenson) 6:31. 4. Canada, Henderson 6:36. 5. USSR, Yakushev (Shadrin) 17:11.
Penalties — Ragulin, 2:09; Lapointe, 8:29; Vasilyev, 8:29; Clarke, 10:12; Hull, 17:02; P. Esposito, 17:46; Canada bench, 17:46.

THIRD PERIOD

No scoring.
Penalty — Ellis, 17:31.

GAME 7 — MOSCOW, SEP. 26, CANADA 4, USSR 3

FIRST PERIOD

1. Canada, P. Esposito (Ellis, Park) 4:09. 2. USSR, Yakushev (Shadrin) 10:17. 3. USSR, Petrov (Vikulov) 16:27. 4. Canada, P. Esposito (Parisé, Savard) 17:34.
Penalties — Mikhailov, 2:00; P. Mahovlich and Mishakov, 5:16; Mishakov, 11:09; P. Esposito, 12:39; White, 15:45.

SECOND PERIOD

No scoring.
Penalties — Gilbert, 00:59; Parisé, 6:04; Anisin, 6:11; P. Esposito and Kuzkin, 12:44; Stapleton, 15:24.

THIRD PERIOD

5. Canada, Gilbert (Ratelle, Hull) 2:13. 6. USSR, Yakushev (Maltsev, Lutchenko) 5:15. 7. Canada, Henderson 17:54.
Penalties — Bergman, 3:26; Gilbert, 7:25; Mikhailov and Bergman, 16:26.

GAME 8 — MOSCOW, SEP. 28, CANADA 6, USSR 5

FIRST PERIOD

1. USSR, Yakushev (Liapkin, Maltsev) 3:34. 2. Canada, P. Esposito (Park) 6:45. 3. USSR, Lutchenko (Kharlamov) 13:10. 4. Canada, Park (Ratelle, Hull) 16:59.
Penalties — White, 2:25; P. Mahovlich, 3:01; Petrov, 3:44; Parisé, 4:10; Tsigankov, 6:28; Ellis, 9:27; Petrov, 9:47; Cournoyer, 12:51.

SECOND PERIOD

5. USSR, Shadrin 0:21. 6. Canada, White (Gilbert, Ratelle) 10:32. 7. USSR, Yakushev, 11:43. 8. USSR, Vasilev (Shadrin) 16:44.
Penalties — Stapleton, 14:58; Kuzkin, 18:06.

THIRD PERIOD

9. Canada, P. Esposito (P. Mahovlich) 2:27. 10. Canada, Cournoyer (P. Esposito) 12:56. 11. Canada, Henderson (P. Esposito) 19:26.
Penalties — Mishakov and Gilbert, 3:41; Vasilev, 4:27; Hull and Petrov, 15:24.

TEAM CANADA

	G	A	P	PM
P. Esposito	7	6	13	15
Henderson	7	2	9	4
Clarke	2	4	6	18
Cournoyer	3	2	5	2
Park	1	4	5	2
Hull	2	2	4	4
Parisé	2	2	4	28
Ratelle	1	3	4	0
Gilbert	1	3	4	9
Ellis	0	3	3	8
F. Mahovlich	1	1	2	0
Perreault	1	1	2	0
Goldsworthy	1	1	2	2
P. Mahovlich	1	1	2	4
White	1	1	2	8
Savard	0	2	2	0
Bergman	0	2	2	13
Cashman	0	2	2	14
Mikita	0	1	1	0
Berenson	0	1	1	0
Lapointe	0	1	1	6
Stapleton	0	0	0	6

USSR

	G	A	P	PM
Yakushev	7	4	11	2
Shadrin	3	5	8	0
Petrov	3	4	7	10
Kharlamov	3	4	7	16
Mikhailov	3	2	5	7
Liapkin	1	4	5	2
Maltsev	0	5	5	0
Lutchenko	1	3	4	0
Anisin	1	3	4	2
Zimin	2	1	3	0
Vikulov	2	1	3	0
Blinov	2	1	3	2
Vasiliev	1	2	3	2
Bodunov	1	0	1	0
Lebedev	1	0	1	2
Gusev	1	0	1	2
Ragulin	0	1	1	4
Tsigankov	0	1	1	4
Kuzkin	0	1	1	8
Mishakov	0	0	0	11

P = Points
P/M = Penalties in Minutes
G = Goals
A = Assists

WE WON !

Last-Second-Henderson Does it Again

THEY STOOD ON GUARD FOR US

September 28, in the fall of 72. We are the winners! The victors are coming home — to Boston, Chicago, New York . . .

"Maple Leaf Gardens . . . home of Paul Henderson," said a sweet little voice answering the 'phone at Harold Ballard's emporium.

Phil Esposito for Pope, suggested one newspaper headline; *Esposito for Prime Minister*, said another. *Paul Henderson could be mayor of Toronto*, aspiring mayor David Rotenberg was reported to have said. *Eagleson in the Senate*, someone remarked, leaving us to wonder whether Ottawa or Washington was meant.

Let the puck replace the maple leaf on our flag, implored a Montreal man-in-the-street, not otherwise identified by a French-language newspaper. An NHL puck?

If Phil were to decline being Pope or Prime Minister, he might make the best leader of the official opposition we've ever had. What with his unique, never-failing, opportunistic scoring skill, he'd make the government take notice of the House. Besides, he's got another qualification. Did he not tell Canadians what he really thought of them, in Vancouver, after Game Four? What real-life politician has ever matched that performance and told us the truth to our faces?

As the final game was televised at lunch-time, eastern judges were reported to have called recesses for unusually long hours. The bastion of Canadian capitalism, Bay street, was deserted while the game was on, and trading on the Stock Exchange fell to a trickle. On the election hustings political campaigns stopped. Mr. Trudeau flew home to Ottawa, watched the last period of the game, and immediately offered *Team Canada* a ceremonius welcome in the nation's capital. Montreal's Mayor Jean Drapeau could do no less in the spirit of *hospitalité-Québec* and *olympism*. Mayor William Dennison of Toronto offered to open the doors of his magnificent City Hall and give the whole team cuff links. In short, everybody who was somebody joined the chorus, as well they should, to welcome the heroes.

Meanwhile, back in Prague, *Team Canada* was getting ready for a final chore. It nearly lost a friendly match against the Czech Nationals, making it an even score 3-3, with seconds to spare.

The mood in Canada was euphoric, ecstatic. It lasted through the weekend with manifestations surpassing those of Centennial Year. In Moscow, the mood was mixed.

Punch Imlach, watching the Russian fans at the final

game, had written, "They finally came alive . . . they caught the fever." According to Soviet commentators, the Russian spectators had been alive and alert all the time, especially to what *Tass* described as, "Deliberate cruelty, used as a means of frightening and neutralizing opponents . . . by visitors who displayed a rich arsenal of underhand blows, fighting, lack of self-control."

On the whole, Russian comment was more restrained than what we read back home. *Pravda*: "The matches between the Soviet and Canadian teams who have something to learn from each other, will contribute to the development of world hockey . . ." Another paper, *Rossiya*, pointing out that the amateur home team had lost to the visiting professionals, said, "It was surely not a bad result after all against powerful opponents, the originators of hockey, men who devote all their time to the game."

The Russians had missed the comment of at least two NHL owners who had said after the end of the games in Canada that 90 minutes on the ice for practice during the season, and golf all summer was no longer the right approach to professional responsibilities on the part of people who earned an awful lot of money in the game.

The New York Times found that the series had pointed up a culture gap. The paper's correspondent in Moscow, Hedrick Smith, reported,

"Behind the headlines of the unexpectedly hard-fought and evenly matched series between *Team Canada* and the Soviet Union, there is a study in cultural contrasts, which points up the vastly different treatment of sports in East and West. The hockey styles of the two teams, their coaches, and their fans bear the imprint of national character and the capitalist and Communist systems that produced them.

"The Russian players were clean-cut, disciplined, phlegmatic and, above all, a team or, as they prefer to call it, a "kollektiv" with swift-passing, smoothly rehearsed pattern plays.

"The Canadian players who arrived in Moscow were, by comparison, long-haired, volatile as bull-fighters and just as inclined to virtuoso performances. Their rough play — the machismo that helps them win fatter pay cheques at home, as one veteran Canadian sportswriter commented — was genuinely unpopular with rule-conscious Muscovites.

"Tall, baldish Russian head coach Vsevolod Bobrov endured the ulcerous tension of the games, expressionless and motionless at his bench, giving minimal instructions, and taking a laconic tone in his post-game comments about the refereeing and the results.

"Dark-haired, young Harry Sinden, the Canadian coach, paced behind the bench like a caged lion, and in post mortems with the press, threw verbal darts at the referees.

"By the time the series ended, advantage *Team Canada* 4-3-1 however, the Soviet Union's players were no longer taking their penalties from the referees with their traditional impassive acquiescence. But they were still mild compared with the Canadian players, who heaved chairs on the ice, or with forward Jean-Paul Parisé who, after what he thought was a bad call, menaced a referee with his hockey stick.

"Warm, emotional and lively in personal relations or in private, the Russians seemed serious, subdued and conformist at the games. In contrast to the raucous Canadian cheering, the Russian chants of "shai-bu" (goal) and "ma-la-tsi" (well done) seemed tame. The trumpets and cowbells of the Canadian stands were as new to the USSR sports scene as the ads painted on the inside of the rinkboards.

"But if the Canadians had surprises for the Russians, the Russians had some for the Canadians, too. The single-minded, almost Calvinistic earnestness of the Russians about sports stunned *Team Canada*.

"When the Russians journeyed to Canada to start the series in early September, it was they who held the Canadian pros in awe. In their neat suits, the Russian players lined up quietly and patiently one by one, getting the autograph of Boston Bruins' famous defenceman, Bobby Orr.

"Even before the series ended, however, the Canadians held some of the Russian players in awe. Many who had predicted an eight-game sweep before the series began, were calling the Soviet Union team the equivalent of *Stanley Cup* competition and ticking off how many Russian players could make the National Hockey League.

"Paradoxically, some Canadians have come away with the impression that in many ways it is the Russians who take the truly professional approach to hockey, more than the stars of the National Hockey League.

"Theoretically, the big difference between the Canadians and Russians is that the latter do not play for pay. It is generally accepted that Russian athletes live well, including apartments, cars and bonuses for good performances in international events. Yet the privileges carry obligations for the Russian players that Western athletes would find confining. For instance, a Soviet Union athlete cannot refuse to compete in an international event. Nor would a Russian athlete do what four unhappy *Team Canada* members did in Moscow — pack their bags and go home."

Also noting the difference between two cultures that have developed opposing teams for "a kind of war, and not entirely bloodless at that," *The Globe and Mail* asked editorially if "this sort of nationalistic team-jousting should be organized again." The paper commented,

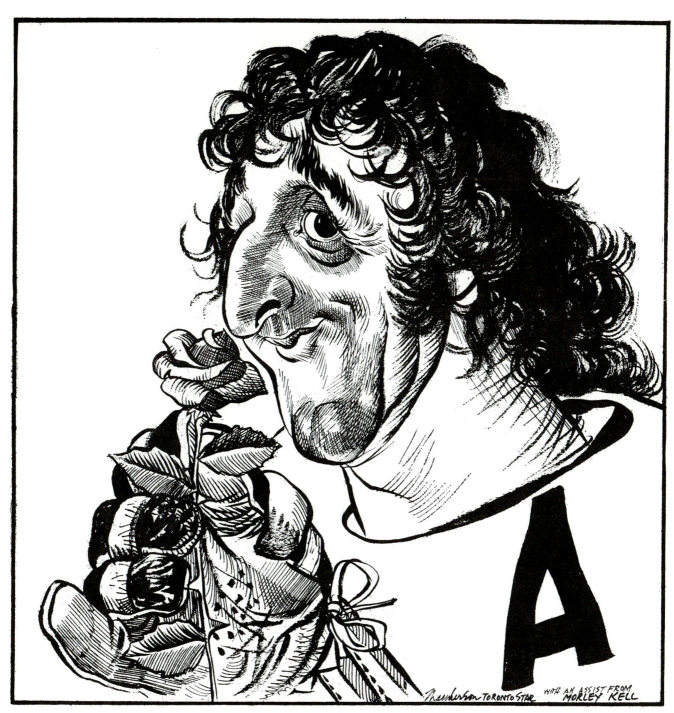

CANADA'S FIRST ITALIAN PRIME MINISTER

"FOR PETE'S SAKE SLEEP AND QUIT SINGING 'O CANADA'..!"

"In its challenge, Soviet Russia was looking for a political triumph. In the assembling of the Canadian team, the commercialism of North American hockey was made crudely apparent.

"After the initial shock of the Russian team's excellence (how many hockey aeons is it since the sports commentators were gleefully predicting an eight-game win for Canada?) the spectacle came to involve Canada's national honour, often in unpleasant ways. There was the booing in Vancouver when the Canadians lost, and the ruthless tactics in Stockholm because Canada's superiority had to be asserted at any cost."

The Globe and Mail's considerations went beyond the spectacle which it had been reporting as a thrilling series of events. It put the question of repeating the series in a political context. The paper's Montreal counterpart, *Le Devoir*, did likewise and concluded that future hockey encounters preferably should be "normalized" international competitions, to be organized under "the proper auspices."

Hockey Canada chairman Douglas Fisher took the question back to spectator interest when he wrote:

"There's been nothing lovely or classical about this *Team Canada* style and method, nothing of the neat grace and pattern shown by fine Montreal Canadien teams or by the USSR. It has been effective. It was symbolized by the persistence and the flicking opportunism of Phil Esposito. It wouldn't have worked if almost every player on every shift had not given total effort and then gotten off the ice, whistle or not, when his zip was gone.

"Part of the "self-psyching" at the core of *Team Canada's* relative recovery in Moscow was the umbrage worked up over refereeing inadequacies and Russian duplicity in masking grievous offences against the Canadians. "Kicking! Holding! Interference!"

"The matter of relative culpability in cleanness or dirtiness of play will be important in prospects for future exchanges between North American pro players and the USSR. At the highest political level in the USSR there is a deep distaste for what they call the barbarianism, the brutal injuring by the Canadians, their open scorn for the referees.

"During the last-hour crisis over referees, at the ministerial level the Russians put it to our government people that our team's brutality was so gross that it was useless to talk about future series. After the series they would have to consider whether future games were a useful experience.

"What the Russian hockey authorities, from ministers down to the coaches, seem not to appreciate is that it has been the very contrast in styles which has made this a uniquely, exciting series. If our team had had the skating speed and passing skills to play a style like the Russians the contrast would have been less.

"If the Russians do not imitate our disregard for puck control and if our players could be persuaded to give over their cheesey histrionics in challenging penalties and referees, the promise of series in the years ahead is really wonderful — at least for fans."

In another analytical comment, part of an editorial, *The Toronto Star* also came down on the side of more engagements in the future. The paper also had this to say under the title "*A triumph of spirit over system.*"

"The lessons taught by the Soviets' shockingly proficient play in the Canadian half of the series still stand up. The myth of the Canadian pros' clear superiority is dead and buried. In at least three elements of the game — conditioning, passing and power-play formation — the Soviets are better. NHL owners and coaches will have to learn from them. After this magnificent series, the NHL won't be able to kid the paying customers of the New York Islanders or the Oakland Seals that they're watching the world's best hockey.

"One lesson was added, or confirmed, in Moscow — that international rules make the game better. Forget the contempt heaped on European referees by our players and sportswriters. The point is not that some of these referees are incompetent, which they are; the point is that their tradition requires them to try to enforce a cleaner, more sportsmanlike standard of play than North American fans are used to. When this code is applied even half-properly, it cuts out much of the clutching and grabbing, roughing and fighting, and compels the players — surprise, surprise to concentrate on hockey. Must Canadians be reminded that that's the name of the game? The effect . . . can be beautiful.

"While in Europe, our team reflected poorly on itself and Canada in only one way — in some players' bull-headed rejection of a different hockey etiquette. They acted as if they had been divinely assured that Canada was right and the world was wrong; they had to be dragged, swinging and cursing, into what must surely be a new and superior era of hockey. Their jawing at referees may have had a wholesomely subversive effect on Soviet fans, by demonstrating disrespect for constituted authority. But their behavior cost them friends in Europe, and it almost cost them the victory.

"Never mind; they'll learn. All of *Team Canada* who played in Moscow earned our gratitude by displaying a splendid, stirring resilience of spirit — a hockey intangible in which they may still be superior to the Soviets.

"They will be rightly hailed as heroes when they return to Toronto Sunday."

Jacques Barrette, writing in *Montréal-Matin* was not so

sure that the winners should be welcomed as heroes. The title of his article is best translated as "an off-colour victory." He deplored the "antics of some of the players and *Team Canada* leadership." And as a true Olympian, he concluded: "Winning is important, but it is not everything . . ." Another Montréalais, Jean Aucoin, wrote in the same newspaper that Canadians should think twice before they permit another "series of the century." "Hide Eagleson from public view and keep him away from hockey . . . tell the spoiled darlings and the fatheads to behave or stay home . . . tell Harry Sinden and his assistant, Frosty Sorepall, that it is absolutely forbidden to throw chairs on the ice . . . and get properly organized and prepared for the next round . . . in order to win more convincingly, and with good manners . . ."

Speaking, without a doubt, for anyone who might consider any viewpoint out of place except the most favourable one, the editorial writer of the *Hamilton Spectator* offered nothing but sweet adulation. He wrote under the title, "No nation could be prouder."

"It's greater than ever to be a Canadian today. And there is one reason for that exultant feeling, one reason alone, the absolutely magnificent display of courage and teamwork by *Team Canada* against the brilliant Soviet hockey team.

"We join millions of other Canadians in congratulating our team for giving fresh meaning to *O Canada* and *The Maple Leaf*. To our players, we must add that their display of team spirit under fire did in a fantastic almost erre way unite Canadians from coast to coast as seldom before in the nation's history."

Deeper down in Ontario, *The London Free Press*, possibly with just a little bit of uneasiness, referred to "national heroics in Moscow," and said,

"Canadian pride in the national game technically has been restored. For that, credit goes to a valiant band of professional hockey players, who refused to be intimidated by the superior game planning and superior conditioning of a Russian team and fought uphill — fuelled, it seemed, on raw patriotism alone — to win the eight-game series.

"There were few Canadian throats without lumps when the final whistle was blown in the Moscow sports palace yesterday. It was a time for emotional nationalism in the arena and the feeling was shared by millions in front of television sets at home."

"How about that!" exclaimed *The Ottawa Journal*. The national capital newspaper, a monument of decorum treasured in the best diplomatic circles, was probably caught up in what it described as "a national roller coaster ride of emotions . . ." In superlatives the paper approved

of the Canadian performance and exalted in the joys felt by Ottawans over the victory. But then, tartly, the writer stated that we had seen a "contest that may make the *Stanley Cup* playoffs bush league by comparison." If that is not an example of ingratitude about which Clarence Campbell complained, then what is? However, no doubt for the benefit of its diplomatic readership, the *Journal* did not want us to forget the Soviets who "have proven beyond all doubt that their players and brand of hockey belong high in the first class . . . deserving the highest degree of respect Canadians and the world can give them."

At least one vocal spoil-sport committed his wrath to paper in the midst of jubilation. John Robertson of *The Montreal Star*, a serious patriot and a thoughtful man, made an angry, bitter attack on *Team Canada* and its leaders. Prime target of his volleys was Alan Eagleson.

The omnipresent, omnipotent Eagleson continued to invite attention. He confided to Bob Hanley of *The Hamilton Spectator* in Moscow, after the last game, "We came out alive. Just imagine, an all-star team, playing out of condition on the other guy's big rink, with a different set of rules and with the other guy's referees. To hell with them and Bunny Ahearne and all the rest. They forced us to play with one hand behind our back. It was a mistake to have come over here under all the conditions . . . I realize that now. Next time we'll be conditioned, and the rules and the referees will be ours."

This kind of attitude and the questions of nationalism and national pride must have weighed heavily on John Robertson's heart when he wrote,

"Okay, I lost my bet — by some 30-odd seconds — but I think I won the point I have been making.

"Rather, Uncle Al Eagleson won it for me with that obscene . . . "Up Yours!" . . . gesture he made to one and all, from centre ice during the third period, as he was being escorted across the ice by security men.

"The gesture was so typical. It said it all for Team Ugly, and it's just too bad they didn't see fit to re-run it in slow-motion, along with J. P. Parisé's threat to cleave that official with his stick. Those were "highlights" of Team Ugly in action, along with coach Harry Sinden and the team trainer throwing chairs onto the ice during the Parisé incident.

"I freely admit blowing my prediction and I bow to the genius of each and every one of you out there who called Canada to win it, four games to three with one tied. What concerns me deeply is that it just could be the most expensive victory, prestige-wise, in the history of Canadian sport.

"Now if you are one who thinks that how we play the game doesn't matter; that anything goes in word, gesture or tactics as long as we score more goals than the other guy; there's no way you'll ever comprehend the point I'm trying to make.

"What is of more consequence? . . . Showing the world what kind of hockey players we produce? Or showing the world what kind of people we produce?

"I sat and stared at that television screen and asked myself this question: If you were watching this from an impartial observer's chair, anywhere in Europe, what conclusions would you draw from the entire series? I looked, and I saw us as a bunch of barbarians, being led by a man who qualifies as a walking diplomatic disaster. Or maybe you would like Canada and all Canadians to be judged by the conduct of this uncouth ass? Maybe you would condone it as just the way Canadians, a very aggressive people, play the game.

"Who really won this series? What did Canada's last-gasp victory prove? That we play the game better than the Russians do? Should that be so surprising? We dominated them so "thoroughly" they outscored us 32-31.

"We didn't really win anything! We merely salvaged something from the wreckage yesterday — something to cling to; so we can say to the world: Well, we may be obnoxious barbarians; we may have come across as the most grotesque, uncouth people ever turned loose in an international athletic forum; we may have undone just about everything our diplomats abroad have been able to do for Canada's image; we may have shown the world we have absolutely no respect for game officials, opposing coaches, or the laws and customs in countries in which we are guests; we may lead the league in both menacing and obscene gestures; but at least we won the damned hockey game.

"Maybe I'm just not the right kind of person to be writing a sports column. Maybe this space should be reserved for some guy sitting in front of the TV set, pounding his fist into the arm of the chair and bellowing: "Kill the bums! Cripple those Commie Rats!" But I can't be that way.

"In the end, I wasn't even rooting for *Team Canada*. I confess I was at the start, even though this is no more our National team than General Motors is our National auto team. It's Team NHL Governors. Team Al Eagleson. Bobby Hull need not apply.

"Representing you and me? Don't be sucked in by that bilge. I was outside *Team Canada*'s dressing room after that loss in Vancouver. I know what Phil Esposito, Brad Park and Bill Goldsworthy think about Canadian hockey fans. They said it bluntly, obscenely in fact — in the old Al Eagleson tradition. Goldsworthy said he was ashamed to be a Canadian. And you know something? I'm ashamed he's a Canadian too. That's when I started rooting for the other side to teach us a lesson.

"Maybe those three wins in Russia clear the books in some people's minds. Not in mine.

"Certainly it was a great, inspirational comeback by *Team Canada*. Nobody is disputing their natural ability — their God-given ability — to play hockey. What I'm complaining about is the way they abdicated an infinitely greater responsibility — as Canadians, carrying Canada's image to untold millions who are going to judge us as people by what they see on television. Never mind the excuses, the piteous moaning about the referees, the excuse that we forgot to shake hands after our first loss because of ignorance, the bleating that those Russians are sneaky, dirty and that our fine upstanding Canadian boys were just retaliating like red-blooded patriots. I saw Phil Esposito give a Russian a vicious two-hander across the back in the corner late in the game — and then raise his arms derisively to the crowd.

"But most of all, I'll remember Uncle Al, the Players' Pal, going out as he came into this whole garish charade, with that gesture which said it all for the kind of individual he would have all the world believe every Canadian is . . . He gave the world the Team Ugly Canada salute . . . "Up Yours!!" "

His editor, Red Fisher, still in Prague when Robertson's article appeared in print and probably unaware of its contents, wrote himself the next day an admiring though not uncritical profile of Alan Eagleson, the man who "put it all together . . . miscast in a villain's role."

Red Fisher's notion, shared by many others, is that without Eagleson the series would not have taken place. He wrote: "Eagleson can go out a winner now if he wishes. But if he does, the game is a loser. So don't go, Al. Not now."

Mr. Eagleson's manners and style have marked the hockey series as much as the conduct of any of the players. It is quite possible that without his efforts *Team Canada* would not have been. But that appears to be exactly the point, or part of the point, which enjoyed a brief debate during the Hull-abaloo. Mr. Eagleson did Canada's bidding in matters far more important than the assembly of *Team Canada*. He acquired or assumed power and authority in a vacuum, as a devoted Canadian citizen, and the agent of a number of NHL players. He was unavoidably and inevitably put in a position where he did not belong. He decided issues and answered questions which were within the province of elected and appointed officials. Think what we will of his contribution and his manners, we cannot ignore the fact that a great many people failed their assignments. Time will tell if they also failed Canada's own, legitimate, important interests of which the hockey series was merely symbolic.
H.W.H.

DEATH OF A LEGEND?

A legend is dead. Or is it?

It was a young legend, vital and prolific. It inspired Canadians with conviction and lent credence to their claim to unrivaled prowess and a measure of the world's attention.

The record of a hockey series can be plotted in statistics; the life of a legend defies such analysis — its origin is as uncertain as its end. Legends do not die; they suffer interruptions or transitions, not a total, final demise.

So, Canada's hockey legend will find new life in other dimensions, in new directions, to give us new illusions. But for the moment we know that we have met a rival — powerful and able who has shaken our conviction of superiority and refuted our claim to pre-eminence. The world may not care that our identity has changed. We know it has, and we care. We know that in the summer of '72 new realities entered our national life. Whether or not they really should matter is not the question. They evidently do concern the majority of Canadians.

We won the series. But the victory itself should be seen for what it was. We nearly lost. Until the very last seconds of the last game, the issue remained in doubt. The Russians scored one more goal than *Team Canada* overall. We deserved to win but so did the Russians. We were the challengers who, at the outset, gave the Russians few odds on winning. They beat us first and then forced us to play their kind of game. They deserved victory as much as we did, or more so, all things considered. They needed to win less than we did; far less, for victories in sports, as in so many other fields, come to the Soviets with habit-forming regularity.

On the ice we made good our claim that "our best" can beat the Russians; not necessarily that "our best" can beat any team, anywhere, anytime. It was great hockey; better hockey throughout the series than many Canadians remember ever having seen before. *Team Canada* met its match and owed the quality of its performance to the quality of the adversary.

Team Canada at times demonstrated flashes of crude and primitive play. Our players had the edge often because of brawn and muscle against a team whose motives were different and whose conduct was constrained by collective discipline and a more stringent code of individual sportsmanship.

Some Canadians' manners were less than admirable but an occasional slip in conduct is tolerated in the best societies. We will be forgiven in this instance because *Team Canada* made up for what it lacked in grace by abundant good spirit, good humor and uninhibited abandon. *Team Canada* displayed bravado and performed the rituals of confrontation in the best tradition of the North American arena. They measured up in combat to the highest expectations of those spectators who have a passion for violence and a simplistic preference for good-guy-bad-guy conflict. (Nice guys finish last, don't they?)

Perhaps the Canadian coaches and the players' mentor, Mr. Eagleson, may have shocked an audience unaccustomed to spontaneous expressions of innermost emotions. But the Russians, who understand the moods and modes of uncomplicated men, whose history and disposition is not devoid of barbarism, were probably less offended than Canadian comment would have us believe. The significance of such incidents as we have seen lies elsewhere. Things said and done in the heat of passion should be considered in the light of the events that provoked them. If adult people with a secure place in life can "forget" themselves outrageously; if time and again we "discover" how great our national anthem sounds, how "unbelievable" it is that we can sing it; if men can say on one occasion that playing for Canada is the greatest thrill in their lives and on the next that they are ashamed to be Canadians, if responsible people in public view and officials in public service can take leave of their senses, then it only confirms and

underlines the fact that the issue was greater, infinitely greater, than the game of hockey. Each and every participant acted out his role in a legend. Each and every instance was a moment in the legend's dying.

We won the games. We lost a legend. On balance, that leaves us little to be cheerful about. We will play games again but, without the legend, they will be games, just games. Our efforts to beg, borrow or steal future Canadian teams will have to contend with reality. Our motives for wanting to play again will have to demonstrate such fundamental desires as winning in a sports contest for which we have prepared as sportsmen and for which we have developed players in large numbers, at many levels, in Canada for Canadians' sake. The old legend, dead or interrupted, will be an inspiration. The rest is housekeeping.

That leaves, as it should, professional hockey to businessmen and entertainers. They have exploited the legend, Canada and Canadians long enough to be satisfied now to return to minding their own affairs, nothing but their own affairs; and to minding them a lot better if they want to stay in business.

As for the rest — Hockey Canada, the government and other assorted interests — they all meddled with the legend and killed it. From now on, let them take care of the mechanics . . . the housekeeping, only.

H.W.H.

The Publishers are grateful for the permission to reprint articles, cartoons and photographs which appeared in:

The Montreal Star The Gazette, Montreal
The Globe and Mail, Toronto The Toronto Star
The Toronto Sun The Ottawa Citizen
The Ottawa Journal The Spectator, Hamilton
The Free Press, London The Edmonton Journal
The New York Times

Photographs appear with permission of and credit to: Boris Spremo (all color and cover), The Toronto Star, Canadian Press, Julien Lebourdais, and World Wide.

This book owes its existence to the following writers: Dick Beddoes, The Globe and Mail, Toronto; Ted Blackman, The Gazette, Montreal; Dennis Braithwaite, The Toronto Star; Jim Coleman, Southam Press; Milt Dunnell, The Toronto Star; Douglas Fisher, The Toronto Sun; Red Fisher, The Montreal Star; Trent Frayne, The Toronto Star; Jack Koffman, The Ottawa Citizen; Frank Orr, The Toronto Star; John Robertson, The Montreal Star; Alexander Ross, The Toronto Star; Hedrick Smith, The New York Times; Jim Vipond and Scott Young, The Globe and Mail, Toronto.

Printed and bound in Canada
Design: Daniel, Knox and Frank

ISBN 0 7730 4008 0